T0356508

# In Praise of *The Motivated Speaker* and Its Authors

"The Motivated Speaker *is a transformative guide for anyone eager to unlock their communication potential. Ruth, Acacia, and Blythe masterfully introduce six threshold principles, offering fresh insights into learning the art of effective speaking. Packed with relatable stories and practical wisdom, this book inspires and empowers readers to become confident, impactful communicators. The lessons and speaker stories felt extremely familiar and are a great motivator!*"

—**Sarah Milks Bethel**
Head of Global Supply Chain
Paula's Choice Skincare/Unilever

"*We turned to the expertise of Articulation to enhance the posit::conf() experience for our 1,500 attendees. Over the past four years, their talents have helped our annual 90+ speakers (no matter their experience level) really upskill their presentations and meaningfully improved the overall conference experience.* The Motivated Speaker *offers a rare chance to learn from these coaches and apply their techniques to elevate your own speaking engagements.*"

—**Hadley Wickham**
Chief Data Scientist
Posit

*"In my years working with Ruth Milligan, both as a speaker coach and co-curator of TEDxColumbus, I've witnessed firsthand her expertise in helping speakers find their voice.* The Motivated Speaker *distills the Articulation team's wisdom into an insightful, practical guide for anyone seeking to become a more effective communicator. Many of the tips I learned from Ruth I use to this day!"*

**—Nancy Kramer**
Founder, Public Board Director, Chief Evangelist
IBM

*"For those without access to a coach,* The Motivated Speaker *is a gift. My work with Acacia taught me to be comfortable in the 'messy' process. The experience had such an impact that I brought Articulation in to help my entire team. I anticipate my copy of the book will be dog-eared and a staple in my speaking tool kit for many years to come."*

**—Dennis Garbarino**
SVP and GM Global Downstream
Nalco Water, an Ecolab Company

*"My coaching from Articulation dramatically changed my entire approach to practicing and presenting my science and making it accessible to any audience. I brought them into my institution, excited for my colleagues to learn the same impactful skills. It's a delight to see so much of their experience now accessible to everyone through this book and these concepts—in the same way we've been enjoying it for the last decade."*

**—Lara McKenzie, PhD, MA, FAAHB**
Principal Investigator
Center for Injury Research & Policy, Abigail Wexner
Research Institute
Nationwide Children's Hospital

"*Practical and endlessly engaging, reading* The Motivated Speaker *felt like being coached by a team of the most compassionate and insightful mentors in the field. The authors have accomplished something remarkable: they've distilled the challenges and joys of public speaking into six transformative concepts that anyone can grasp and apply.*"

**—David Staley, PhD**
Associate Professor
The Ohio State University

"*I reached a point in my career when I realized that continued growth was not just about being an expert in my domain, but also my ability to compel others to believe in an idea, strategy, vision, opportunity. Working with Ruth on the principles outlined in this book not only helped turn my words into ideas worth telling, but her insight moved my words from just being heard to being remembered.*"

**—Stephanie Domas**
Speaker, Author, and Chief
Information Security Officer
Canonical

"*This book is a must-read for anyone looking to conquer the public speaking stage—whether you're a rookie finding your voice or a seasoned speaker who's maybe just a little too confident (like I was before working with these amazing authors). Packed with sharp insights and practical tips, it's a fast track to unlocking your full potential and truly owning the spotlight.*"

**—Tim Raderstorf, DNP, RN, FAAN**
President
Raderstorf Consulting

"*Any speaker looking to improve their communication skills would benefit from the concepts in this book. Despite my extensive public speaking experience as a Senator, CEO, and Governor of Guam, I gained valuable insights from the experience of being coached by Acacia for a TED-like talk. Her guidance helped me embrace my storytelling abilities.*"

**—Hon. Lourdes A Leon Guerrero**
Governor
State of Guam

"*Accessible to both novice and experienced speakers alike,* The Motivated Speaker *clearly and succinctly highlights what makes speaking before an audience a challenging yet rewarding adventure. It delineates the individual elements of preparing and presenting speeches and offers practical advice to increase one's aptitude and influence. The text is punctuated with scores of authentic examples of the troubles and triumphs experienced by speakers. Short of taking a college course in public speaking, this book will get you closer to your speaking goals.*"

**—Paul Mongeau, PhD**
Professor
Hugh Downs School of Human Communication
Arizona State University

"*Having worked and collaborated with the Articulation team for nearly two decades, I continue to be blown away by their versatility, creativity, and relentless spirit of innovation. The art of communication is ephemeral and ever shape-shifting. This book offers a needed road map for anyone navigating today's communications.*"

**—Laurie Kamerer**
Former VP of Communications
Victoria's Secret

"*An engaging, accessible, and informative look at what it takes to be an effective speaker—so relevant as we seek to retain human communication and connection in a world increasingly driven by technology. The stories 'from the trenches,' culled from the authors' years of experience, bring the concepts alive and help ground the reader's understanding. If you're interested in delivering better, more compelling presentations,* The Motivated Speaker *is a must-have resource."*

**—Betsy Allen**
Writer, Editor, and English Instructor
James Madison University

*"Ruth and her team have proven that you can learn to be a great speaker no matter when you start in your career. This book gives you a front row seat to how they draw the best out of anyone wanting to be an impactful communicator."*

**—Edward O'Reilly**
Partner
Citadel

"The Motivated Speaker, *which realigns the mindsets and practices of becoming a great communicator, should be required reading for any speaker. I'll put it on my shelf between Dale Carnegie and Chris Anderson. I can also celebrate the origin of this work on our campus from a chance connection between Dr. Wardle and the authors, two of whom are enthusiastic alums. For all of them and this brilliant manuscript, I can only add a resounding* … love and honor!"

**—Mackenzie Rice**
President
Miami University Foundation

*"While I wish I had this book for the younger me, it couldn't be more relevant and useful. With less time than ever to convey ideas and responses or make connections, these threshold concepts are essential for any speaker."*

**—Geraldine Weiser**
Executive Director Client
Solutions and Programs
Global Corporate College

*"Working with Ruth and her team at Articulation to prepare for a TEDx event transformed the way I approach public speaking. They helped me distill my core message, ensuring it would resonate with the audience. Together, we restructured the presentation into a compelling narrative that made the message more impactful from my opening breath until I exhaled to the sounds of the audience clapping wildly. My time with Articulation not only changed the most important speech of my life that day but every speech that followed."*

**—Larry Smith**
Author, Speaker, and Founder
The Six-Word Memoir Project

*"In my role, I invite physicians, scientists, and scholars to translate their leading-edge work to broad audiences of potential supporters and advocates. I've been a longtime client and champion of Articulation's work in helping with this effort, and this book allows me to keep their thinking and counsel at close reach."*

**—Patty Hill-Callahan**
VP for Advancement
Mount Saint Mary's University

*"This is a powerful and brilliant guide for all who seek to communicate and be communicators. Effective speaking is not necessarily natural— just like anything of substance, it is a craft to be honed through habit and intention. The authors have created a framework from their extensive experiences that should be read and re-read."*

**—J. Nwando Olayiwola, MD, MPH**
Physician, Author, and Speaker
Senior Vice President, Advocate Health

# THE
# MOTIVATED
# SPEAKER

RUTH MILLIGAN
ACACIA DUNCAN
BLYTHE COONS

# THE MOTIVATED SPEAKER

## SIX PRINCIPLES TO UNLOCK YOUR COMMUNICATION POTENTIAL

WILEY

Published by John Wiley & Sons, Inc., Hoboken, New Jersey.
Published simultaneously in Canada.

For general information on our other products and services or for technical support, please contact our Customer Care Department within the United States at (800) 762-2974, outside the United States at (317) 572-3993 or fax (317) 572-4002.

Wiley also publishes its books in a variety of electronic formats. Some content that appears in print may not be available in electronic formats. For more information about Wiley products, visit our website at www.wiley.com.

*Library of Congress Cataloging-in-Publication Data is Available:*

ISBN 9781394338030 (Cloth)
ISBN 9781394338054 (ePDF)
ISBN 9781394338047 (ePub)

Cover Design: Wiley
Cover Image: © Jozef Micic/Shutterstock
Author Photos: © Picture the Love/Kimberly Rottmayer

SKY10100187_031525

*To the speakers who have given us their trust*
*and who continue to inspire us.*

# Contents

# The Spark

In 2023, Dr. Elizabeth Wardle, PhD, the esteemed director of the Howe Center for Writing Excellence at Miami University, delivered a talk to a group of Miami women alumni. It was a Saturday in May right after classes finished for the year, and this event was designed to spark curious graduates with ideas that Miami faculty and staff had been exploring. Ruth was in the audience and also giving the keynote address for the event on best practices for being a great communicator.

That day, Dr. Wardle opened her talk by asking, "When was the last time you wrote something in general for no one in particular?" Even a grocery list is a form of writing, she demonstrated. The list you put together for your spouse may have descriptions of the kind of potatoes you want: two dozen, small, red. You are *mediating their activity* toward buying the right kind of potatoes you want for dinner. If you just wrote "potatoes" they may come home with one of those jumbo bags of tater tots.

Dr. Wardle explained how anyone can be taught how to write, not just those who are English majors. Math majors

1

write proofs, computer scientists write code, supply-chain majors write procedures, construction systems majors write requests for information and change orders. We learned her life's work was re-engineering *how you teach writing* in part using a theory called threshold concepts. Dr. Wardle explained how she taught faculty from across the university how to integrate writing into their specific curricula.

According to Erik Meyer and Ray Land, the researchers who coined the term, "A **threshold concept** can be considered as akin to a portal, opening up a new and previously inaccessible way of thinking about something. It represents a transformed way of understanding, or interpreting, or viewing something without which the learner cannot progress."[1]

Think for a moment about cooking. What do you have to understand in order to actually cook? We think of two things initially: cooking requires heat, and cooking requires ingredients that interact. Neither of those ideas are *what you do* to cook, but without understanding each of them, you won't be a good cook. And they have multiple implications and interactions, all of which contribute to the success *of actually cooking*. If you burn cookies, you will reflect on your understanding of how heat contributed to the outcome. But if the cookies didn't rise properly, you would lean on your understanding of the ingredients you used. It is that understanding AND doing that brings clarity and permanence to the learning.

Threshold concepts, according to Meyer and Land, are:

- both ways of thinking and practicing
- transformative and likely irreversible: we change as a result of them

- troublesome: we struggle when we learn them
- necessary: if we want to move forward in an area, like speaking, they are concepts we must encounter
- recursive: we encounter them again and again and perhaps learn something different each time they are encountered
- integrative: they allow us to perceive connections between concepts and ideas
- challenging enough that learners may exist in a liminal space while they seek to understand them.[2]

Ruth came back from the event totally sparked. It made her want to interrogate what the corollary threshold concepts are for *learning to speak*. So she posed this question to the team at Articulation at the following Monday meeting:

*"When was the last time you said something in general to no one in particular?"*

Aside from the mumbling you may do as you crawl through a morning routine before caffeine, every time we speak, we do so with the intention to share knowledge, entertain, influence, or persuade.

For nearly 15 years, our firm, Articulation, has fielded calls from thousands of people like you asking us to help improve your speaking, and the speaking of your executives, your leaders in training, and your teams. We have assembled a huge toolkit of effective activities and exercises we use to help you and your leaders build better skills. We know how to make you uncomfortable by listening to your own voice, and recording and watching yourself on video to help you determine what you really want to improve. We also help large conferences prepare their speakers to level up the audience engagement and resonance of thousands of workshop and keynote talks. We coach in little steps, knowing that big change all at once is very hard. Our focus spans structured thinking, storytelling, style and delivery, executive presence—all leading toward ideal congruence between the vocal, verbal, non-verbal, and emotional traits. When these elements come together, speakers become compelling communicators who make an impact, whether it's winning a pitch, getting buy-in for a new strategy, changing hearts, or moving others to action.

But until now, we haven't really understood threshold concepts and their role in both *understanding* and *doing* that enable you to be a good speaker. In parallel, we came to the perhaps obvious but not often articulated conclusion that there is indeed a difference between being a great communicator and crafting a great communication.

So we got to work and with Dr. Wardle's help, we studied, sorted, tested, and narrowed down to six threshold concepts that apply to public speaking. We digested the book she co-authored, *Naming What We Know*, which informed our concepts. There of course is a clear connection between writing and speaking, but her book and this work also help to clarify the unique attributes of each. For the better part of a year, we also shared these six concepts with clients, blogged about them, wrote posts and emails to test if they "stuck" with not only our clients and followers, but also with us.

We now wonder how we've come this far without them. Every time we coach a speaker, design a class, deliver a training, we are calling back to these six concepts. Every time a talent executive calls about a leader who needs development, they unknowingly start with a story that demonstrates that the speaker fundamentally missed one of the concepts in learning to practice and prepare.

During this study, we have come to deeply embrace all six. We believe that if you practice the rituals, habits, and patterns associated with them, we can nearly guarantee you will be a better speaker.

We are intensely proud to present this work and book as a collaboration. When we began the work there was never a mention of a book as an outcome. But we hope as you read it you'll realize this is more than just a book of our thoughts; it's a book with true guidance, especially for those who were not granted access to any form of public speaking teaching, training, or coaching. It is also for those who did have access but not much practice, feedback, or chance to improve.

By the time you finish this book, we hope you will come to understand the necessity and power of a threshold concept in learning anything, and especially these six for learning to be a speaker and communicator. We are indebted to Dr. Wardle for unknowingly sparking our curiosity for ourselves, and now in turn, as a service to you. We know and believe everyone can become a great speaker if you just take a moment to learn . . . how best to learn.

To that end, here's how to understand this book—what it is and what it isn't.

This book is for people who are motivated to become great verbal communicators. It's not the only book you need. But it is the one you've been missing. It will explain the threshold concepts that you will need to encounter and wrestle with to become a great speaker, presenter, panelist, and more. The threshold concepts will not teach you these things, but they are elements necessary for learning.

This book is *not* designed to explain great *communication*, like how to engineer a talk, organize a story, and distill data into insights. We have assembled our best resources of books that address content at the end of the book.

We distinguish between communicator and communication since there are distinct dispositions, mindsets, behaviors, and skills that are required to be an effective communicator regardless of your verbal or spoken communication. That is why this book keeps the speaker and the speaker experience at the center of our narrative.

Many scholars before us identified public speaking as the intersection of **verbal** (what you say), **vocal** (what it sounds like), and **non-verbal** (what you look like when you say it). We will argue a fourth prong: **emotional,** how you are feeling (inside and out) when you are speaking. This drives your disposition, mindset, and ultimately, ability to control your stress response. We will reference all four of these throughout the concepts.

And, as we shared, understanding threshold concepts can forever change the way a person thinks and behaves. To that end, after each concept, we share some best practices—mindsets and strategies that can help you incorporate the threshold.

After the concepts, we briefly spell out the most important skills that you will need to build on your communicator's journey. In this way you can use the threshold concepts to inform your practice of each skill.

We also attempt to address the use of slide visuals. We recognize that, since PowerPoint was developed in 1987, smart thinkers, strategists, and designers have written many books on slide design. *Our* focus is on what an audience needs to see when also listening to someone speak. Because the brain really won't let you both listen and read at the exact same time.

Very few secondary schools teach public speaking or sponsor debate clubs, while college requirements for speech communication have greatly diminished. Companies don't often have a Toastmasters chapter (where speaking can be practiced) or consider core speaking skills in training and leadership programs. The gig economy and working from home has relegated speaking to a tiny camera into a video conference thumbnail window, which is in and of itself an entirely new genre of presentation.

To that end, we have included very practical tips for individuals, educators, and corporate executives alike who teach or manage people. Maybe this will come as a surprise, but developing these threshold concepts has taught us that the same rules for learning to speak apply whether you are a tenth grader or "grade level" ten at a company.

In an election year, a key headline about Vice President Kamala Harris was, "Can she handle an unscripted interview?" meaning at the time, she was yet untested in the genre of *spontaneous* vs. *scripted* speaking. One could argue it was President Biden's speaking performance at his only debate with former President Trump that solidified the lack of confidence in his candidacy. Trump is now known for "the weave" of his narrative, in and out of clarity. Clear, compelling speaking is still the most visible and reliable sign of clear thinking, leadership, empathy, understanding, and problem solving.

Meanwhile, the other daily headlines that continue to dominate are about AI, but it will be many moons before AI will physically speak for a person. We agree there are some effective and ethical uses of AI that we will outline. And while technology tools are advancing quickly, we also have specific recommendations on how to think about using them for improving, practicing, and getting more refined feedback when you speak.

Speaking genres, audiences, messages, channels, goals, and outcomes will be different with every single communication. But being a great communicator takes the same patterned, habitual practice. Welcome to that practice.

## About Us

We are full-time executive communication coaches practicing together in the same Columbus, Ohio–based enterprise, Articulation. Ruth has a background in speechwriting, public relations, and communications consulting; Acacia and Blythe have backgrounds in business and training while both of them are also deeply rooted with both degrees and practice in theater as actors, writers, and directors. We write from the front-row seat that is our daily work, engaging with executives of all levels, walking alongside their struggles and celebrating their successes that are both a necessary part of being a great communicator.

## Authors' Notes:

We interchange the words "speaker" and "communicator" throughout the book. We know when speaking you are always communicating; but when communicating it may not be a formal speech or talk. And sometimes you are doing both in one setting: giving a prepared talk (speaking) and then answering questions (communicating). So we've agreed to use both terms, but please know they are interchangeable depending on the audience, event, genre, venue, and goal.

You will also notice we use the word "talk" throughout the book when referring to working with a speaker. In our practice we use "talk," "speech," and "presentation" interchangeably when discussing any consequential moment where a speaker is delivering a message in front of an audience.

It was very difficult for us to not end up writing a book just about storytelling, a central focus of our work. While we address story structures in Principle #2, we decided to keep our focus on the process a communicator must practice to get to great storytelling. We reference several resources throughout the book to help those interested in storytelling as a stand-alone subject.

*(continued)*

*(continued)*

The book is written from the collective voice of the three of us. However, in order to make the threshold concepts more concrete, we have chosen to share numerous stories from decades of coaching a wide variety of speakers. Names, genders, organizations, and other identifying details have been changed to maintain the anonymity of our clients.

■ ■ ■

## The Threshold Concepts for Public Speaking

Speaking is habitual (not natural)

Speaking is messy

Speaking is social

Speaking contains multiple genres

Speaking is embodied

Successful speaking requires feedback

# 1

# Speaking Is Habitual

It's awfully convenient to think speaking is natural. If you're not that great, that's okay. As in, some people have "it" and others don't.

But that's entirely untrue.

No one is born speaking.

And while your capacity for language development grows with age, you don't learn it without another human speaking to you. As a quick primer and evidence, here are the key steps we all experience from birth:

**Listening and Imitation:** Babies attempt to imitate sounds they hear. *Mama*, *dada*, a dog's name—all things they hear often or are taught to say first.

**Social Interaction:** Parents and caregivers are the first teachers of talking, singing, reading out loud, and of course, screaming and yelling.

**Feedback and Reinforcement:** When babies attempt to make sounds or words, what do parents and caregivers do? Ignore them? Hardly! They smile, talk back, ask more, and most importantly, provide encouragement to keep trying.

**Exposure to Language:** The more words a baby hears, the more they are influenced toward language development. Dare we say also, if they are in a French-speaking household, they most certainly will not learn, say, German.

**Cognitive Development:** As the brain develops, so does the capacity for more understanding and language production.

Okay, enough brain science for today.

But . . . but . . . "That person is such a *natural-born speaker*," you may say.

"They were not born one," we say.

Babies start with gurgling sounds, and then move onto babbling, eventually uttering distinguishable words usually around a year old. Even as adults, we are still learning new words all the time. No matter our age, we are always listening to others and learning from them, from our parents at birth to our leaders in our careers. And as we learn, we practice, and this builds our habits.

That's why the threshold concept is that speaking is habitual. We believe speaking is learned and practiced, not natural—even when it's something you do without thinking.

A speaker who hasn't yet encountered or embraced the threshold concept of trying to build a new habit will not work their way into better habits.

Let's make this concrete with a story. One habit that many people carry is too many filler words (*ums, like, you know*), trite phrases or other "disfluencies" that get in the way of being heard. Ruth worked with a client with such vocal patterns. This (true) story illustrates how critical it is that a speaker wrestles with this first threshold concept:

**Ruth:** So . . . I'm engaged by your company to help with speaking effectiveness, especially for this pitch. By chance do you know you are an "ummer"?

**Client:** Uh. What's an ummer?

**Ruth:** Someone who says UM, UH, YOU KNOW, RIGHT?, LIKE a lot . . . They are what we call "disfluencies." Or filler words. Or things that get in the way of us hearing your message.

**Client:** Ummmm . . . that's just how I talk. Are you saying I do that a lot?

**Ruth:** Yes. A lot.

**Client:** Really? I do? (In disbelief.)

**Ruth:** Well, I counted 23 times in a three-minute response to a question. On the phone last week, I heard it every three to four words. I didn't hear it once today—but that's because you were reading your prepared script.

*Fast forward a few days to another session. Shoot! Ugh. The ummer is still umming. He didn't hear Ruth. Or do what she suggested, which was a specific breath exercise to begin to get in a better habit and out of the ums.*

**Ruth:**   Did you listen to the recording?

**Client:**  Once I did. (Not convincingly.) But I should again probably. But I did try a more conversational style, did that help?

**Ruth:**   So sorry. I wish I could say they are the same. While a "conversational style" and disfluencies are for sure cousins in the spectrum of speaking, they are distinctly different. One is a casual approach to word choice (as in using colloquial, not formal language) and the other is a pile of boulders sitting between you and your audience.

*And. Sigh. Back to square one. But this is what keeps us in business.*

Ruth's speaker suffered from the dreaded ums, and they were getting in the way of being heard. More often than not, ums are a result of a person verbalizing *while* they are thinking. Speakers vocalize as they cover that thinking process, and perhaps subconsciously let the audience know they are not done. Eventually the ums become a habit. A bad one.

We taught this speaker a specific breathing tactic to get rid of the ums, but he hadn't practiced it and therefore, he was still showing up with them. While he understood the *declarative knowledge* (or said he did) about how to get rid of them (the breathing tactic), he ignored the *procedural knowledge* about how to apply the learning (the process for working breath into speech to replace the ums). That's the habit part.

One of our clients aptly said:

> *"You diagnosed pretty quickly and easily what I need to change to do better. But damn if it isn't incredibly hard to do it."*

*Exactly.* Habits are hard work—both to form and break.

As human language progresses from babble to the geography bee to the corporate business review, there is endless learning and training of the brain. We've offered but one example of a hundred different small skills that require practice and habit.

Even the most seasoned keynote speaker is learning about a new audience, new host, new venue, new message every time they speak.

Even if they seem natural, they always have more to learn.

## Know What You Did to Be an Effective Communicator (Then Make It Your Habit)

In Ruth's first year of coaching TEDx speakers, she watched how eight speakers took the stage with incredibly different preparation paths and habits. The preparation of two particular speakers and their different results really stood out to her.

One of the speakers went away to a silent retreat for three days to write his talk. He spent time brainstorming, writing, editing, probably starting over, and doing it all again. Another one showed up with two talks condensed into one deck that made the talk twice the suggested length, and . . . with no focus. She didn't consider what her *one* idea really was, let alone how to best support it. There were a lot of good thoughts and visuals, but nothing threading them together. Results reflected their disparate preparation journeys. One had done the hard work of the "logic and thinking" of the talk. The other hadn't. It didn't stop there, as the one who didn't do the hard work had a talk double the time and even harder to follow.

Ruth saw first-hand how the habits (or lack thereof) in preparation impacted the outcome not only for these two speakers, but all eight who took the stage that year. Only a few of them could *reflect in hindsight* what worked or didn't work for them.

Two years later, still coaching TEDx speakers, Ruth wrote a guide with a colleague and TEDxOhioStateUniversity longtime advisor, Dr. Amy Barnes, called "How to be a TEDx speaker coach" based on the specific *procedural steps* that they saw were successful in coaching somebody for the short-form talk. Amy and Ruth were attempting to make sure students could coach faculty members for the student-run event and wanted them to have some tools to be successful (because what tenured faculty member wants to take coaching from a student?).

After that guide was written, we kept hearing speakers say "I will never present the same way again after giving this talk." Mind you, they weren't all TEDx talks, but any talk that needed organization, story, and practice.

In hindsight, writing the guide gave us clarity on what really worked and didn't. In general, we outlined four coaching sessions plus a rehearsal, the specific development goals we had for each call, and various forms of feedback at each step. As a result, the speakers *didn't just succeed, they actually knew what they did to succeed.*

Our role was to be their accountability partners, helping them to know where to edit, stay within time, bring inflection to the mundane, and cheer them on for each step closer they got to an embodied talk. *(We'll address this in Principle #5.)*

And after coaching thousands of speakers over the last 15 years, we can confidently predict the large procedural tasks you will need to complete a great talk to your audience in a specific genre—but your specific habits will be uniquely yours.

Knowing the specific habits you need to form to become a great communicator will usually come from immediate reflection *after a talk.*

But in speaking, sometimes you walk off stage and you have no idea what you just said.

Or perhaps you came off stage and it seemed to go well.

*In both cases you may not appreciate what you did to get to those outcomes.*

This lesson applies to any sorts of speaking moments, not just presentations. We want to help you become an effective communicator in every arena. Reflection after any communication will help you identify what worked and what didn't. In this next story, Acacia was working with a client on a conversation that leaders have all the time, which made it especially important for the client to identify what made her successful in the moment.

## Acacia: Discovering What Matters

While most of our work is helping clients prepare for planned presentations, sometimes we find ourselves helping them with more interpersonal genres of communication. I was working with a long-time client who was preparing for a performance review with one of her staff members, a person we'll call Tony.

It seemed that Tony had been withholding information, only raising his hand for help when things were urgent. This was causing a cascade of problems, and not a small amount of additional stress for my client.

My client knew she had to have a tough conversation, a yearly 360 review, but had some trepidation to go with it. These kinds of talks with Tony had not always been easy or had the desired outcomes. Her previous approach just didn't work—she needed to build a new habit.

In the past, my client had focused on the information she wanted to share in her employee reviews. So this time, as we prepared for the conversation, we focused primarily on what the goal was. We investigated what she needed to come from the conversation. What actions did she need to see from Tony?

And then we thought about Tony. Was this going to be new information for Tony? What has changed in his world? What did he want to get out of the conversation?

Then I asked my client: What is the most important thing that needs to happen in the meeting? She paused, looked down at her notebook, and then slowly said, "I need him to trust me." No matter what happened in the meeting, I encouraged her to keep that goal front and center.

A month after the 360 review, I grabbed another call with my client and asked, "How did it go?"

She smiled and said, "Better than I could have hoped." She proceeded to tell me how she had learned that Tony had some outdated information that he was working from. Once they cleared that up, they were able to come to an agreement about his behavior. And he had kept his word, reaching out proactively. Bonus, he had become an employee she looked forward to talking to.

As I celebrated with her, it was important that we focused on what she did that gave her this positive outcome. New habits need to be reinforced after all. I asked, "What made the biggest difference in the success of the conversation?"

She told me that it was remembering that she was trying to build trust. She kept focusing on that goal. From then on, she made sure to determine what really mattered before she walked into any conversation. And this new habit serves her well.

The truth is, while having a coach to aid you in your new habit formation is really helpful, you don't *need* one to ask you these questions. We have some tips at the end of the chapter to help build a habit of reflection into your practice.

## Your Changing Audience Requires Continuous Learning (and New Habits)

No two audiences are the same. Even if they are the same people, they have had different experiences between the times you spoke to them. They have inevitably learned more, encountered different challenges and the world around them has changed as well.

Every audience brings diverse experiences (and some baggage) to their listening, and the stakes are always different.

No matter how many times you give the same talk, it will always need to be adjusted to suit the audience in front of you. For each audience or genre (more to come on both of these topics), no matter how similar they may seem, it's important to go back and investigate them.

We have a favorite moment with speakers when we begin an engagement. If they come to the first coaching call with a slide deck from an old talk, we gently say:

> *"Who is this deck for? Is your new audience exactly like your old one? Do they have the same context, same questions, same problems to solve?"*

The old slide deck usually gets set aside, maybe never to be seen again.

We extensively work in what we call "deep knowledge fields" with researchers, scientists, and data analysts. When we nudge (or shove) them out of their lab to speak to "lay audiences," it is a lift. While we really love clients like the molecular investigators, they are tough. Their work supports other scientists and rarely do they communicate with "folks not in their lab." They want to stay deep inside molecular science and their outcomes are also, well, molecularly based. But when they speak to audiences without this background, none of this works. They need to try new strategies. And they need to learn to connect molecules to people. This is opposed to an outcome that sounds like "curing diabetes." Their work may end up there but trying to articulate the many steps in between is the work that takes effort for that new, unanointed audience.

Particularly for young academics, they can become so focused on perfecting the academic talk that when we show up to help them prepare for a new group of listeners, things can go awry, like Blythe shares here.

### Blythe: Continuous Learning for Academics

Not that long ago, I worked with a wonderful group of academics: international, in diverse fields of research, and really smart. They'd been chosen to participate in a speaker showcase. The event was designed to be a "TED-like" event and billed as such for the audience. They were expecting enlightening, fun, story-filled talks.

The request for talks was not specifically themed around ideas from their fields or their research. They could talk about anything! Of course, they all chose to speak about their research, because they were most comfortable with the content they knew best.

*(continued)*

(*continued*)

Everything was going well.

Until . . .

We got to the coaching session where they give a really rough version of their talks for the first time. This is undoubtedly the hardest session for speakers in any field, because it reveals their comfort level for sharing their ideas out loud, and their ability to convey those ideas in language the average person outside their labs and fields would understand.

There was one student, Rose, who spent a bulk of her speaking time establishing her license to influence. She listed her impressive but wordy accomplishments, and then basically ran out of time to spend on the main content. As a burgeoning academic, this was the habit she had built to ensure that her academic peers took her seriously. She didn't need the same license to influence this audience.

I should have guessed that she, and all of them, would struggle. This was the first time in their grad program that they were asked to speak to a much more general audience in a different genre of talk (more on genre in Principle #4). Rose had chosen a very formal structure: problem statement, supporting statistics, solution. This problem/solution talk style (see Principle #2) was her habit and what felt most familiar to her. But that's not what she was asked to do in these circumstances. Her audience expected something totally different, and Rose would need new habits to get there.

So we had to back up a little bit. Rethink the content given new inputs.

I began to see Rose stretch herself in the lead up to the event. Unsurprisingly, she turned out to be a very quick study. She learned about the power of stories, even in supporting research, and how to craft stories that make sense and captivate. She learned a new way of structuring her ideas for a talk. She learned that examples can sometimes be more important than statistics. She learned how to bring herself into her research and found out it can feel a little vulnerable. Most importantly, she learned that there are different ways to share her information with different audiences so they can hear her more clearly.

Rose is lucky to have encountered this threshold early in her career. It's unlikely she will forget the experience soon; she and her colleagues got a lot more than they were expecting when they were chosen for this event.

But this story is not just about young people, or exclusively about academics. It's just one example of how we all have room to learn and build new habits each time we communicate with a new audience.

## Habits → Trust = Confidence

At the beginning of almost every engagement with a speaker, whether we are coaching individually or facilitating group training, we always ask: "What do you want to get out of our time together?"

Inevitably one word bubbles to the surface: *confidence.*

"*I want to* appear *more confident.*"
"*I want to* sound *confident.*"
"*I want to* feel *confident.*"
"*I want more confidence.*"

Don't we all. But coaching and training "to confidence" is tricky because a coach or a workshop can only do so much.

In this case it helps to get a little nerdy and think about the root of the word, *confidence*, which comes to English from Latin.

At the center of confidence is "fidere," which means *to trust.* So confidence means *to give trust.* In the mid-15th century, it came to mean a "reliance on one's own powers, resources, and circumstances."[1]

So for speakers, we contend that to "feel confident" is to give yourself trust.

Emma Hayes, the coach of the US Women's National Team, received the highest coaching honor, the Ballon d'Or, as the Women's Soccer Coach of the Year. One TV commentator reporting on the award said, "What makes Emma such a great coach is that she trusts herself, which allows her to trust her team."[2]

"Just trust yourself" is advice that is far from helpful and not easy for many speakers.

Giving yourself trust is instead a process, an action (or series of actions) that you take; the end result is confidence. We invite our clients who want to build their confidence to think about what they need to *do* to trust in their own power, resources, and circumstances.

That's why we're talking about confidence in this chapter on habits. Your confidence will in large part rest on the habits that you build.

What habits of preparation allow you to trust that you have done enough?

What type of practice allows you trust in your ability to pivot and recover when things go wrong?

What have you learned after each time you speak, and, critically, how have you applied those lessons?

Knowing that you have a robust set of habits around your speaking that includes the threshold concepts will help you to go into any presentation with confidence.

*An additional note on looking/sounding confident:*

*We believe that the foundation of the appearance of confidence is actual confidence built over time. However, there are some vocal habits (like ums, soft-speaking, and going up at the end of sentences [upspeak]) and non-verbal clues (like poor posture, pacing, or lack of eye-contact) that can get in the way and indicate an unsure or self-conscious speaker. These poor habits need to be identified and replaced with solid skills that allow your confidence to shine. (See Core Skills.)*

### Takeaway

Even for the most practiced speaker, there is always more to learn. Speaking is not just plug-and-play. Being willing and open to learning *and* re-learning is the only way to improve, and adapting to audience expectations and audience interests is paramount to success.

# Best Practices for Building a Good Speaking Habit

As you wrestle with any of these principles, consider an encouraging mantra.

This is one we often say for habit:

**"Keep moving forward."**

Wherever you are, take one step closer to where you want to be. This is particularly helpful with speakers who show up to coaching calls unprepared. In those moments we say: let's use this time to help you get to where you need to be. It is a disarming philosophy, both for those who are always too busy to make time to work before a call, and for those who expect to be perfect (which doesn't exist). Neither of those approaches help in forming good habits, so we teach them how to do so on each call.

There are a couple of key dispositions or mindsets that help along the way.

## Be a Learner: Always Be Willing to Improve

No matter how advanced or seasoned a speaker is, we know they always have something to improve upon. Namely because every audience, every event, every story can change from talk to talk. And so do our bodies, our voices, our energy, and stamina.

The disposition to be a continuous learner is directly tied to the concept of speaking being habitual. You must be curious and eager to learn if you intend to create and recreate habits that support you.

It's also closely tied to feedback, which we will discuss in Principle #6. Receiving feedback can be hard, especially if you see it as an evaluation of your worth as a speaker. But, if you maintain a growth mindset and see feedback as an opportunity to improve, you will be a better speaker because of it.

One way you can reinforce this disposition is to ask yourself, after every time you speak: What went well? And what could be even better if . . . ?

### Know Yourself and Build a Preparation Plan (Checklist!)

Like a habit, a plan does not come naturally. Getting a handle on what you need to prepare, how much practice is needed, and what feedback to receive and incorporate is something you have to work at.

Agility in your plan will help you flex with the changing goals, audiences, and genres of your communications. Winging it is not a strategy that leads to influence or success. Also, knowing what you want to work on is central to improving every time you start.

There is no "cramming" in learning to be an effective communicator. Building a strong habit requires

(*continued*)

(*continued*)

*small starts and consistent attempts.* These tips will help you reflect on your habit so you know what works or what doesn't for you.

We pull inspiration from Atul Gawande, surgeon and author of the *Checklist Manifesto*. Gawande was charged with reengineering the process of "surgery" for the World Health Organization, to find efficiencies and also bring more equity to all voices in the surgery process. For example: he observed nurses often had important things to say but doctors weren't interested in their messages or being held accountable by people who weren't perceived as having influence.

The result of his study revealed that a critical checklist before you perform surgery and then a second one at the conclusion had dramatic effects on outcomes. The idea is that you need reminders both before and after, and they are different. Checking to make sure your surgery equipment is clean before you begin is different from checking to make sure you didn't leave an instrument inside someone's body cavity before you stitch them up.[3]

In speaking, our "before you take the stage checklist" might consist of statements like:

☐ I understand that this speaking engagement will take time and I can commit to the time it will take. (For a new talk, you can expect to spend at least one hour in preparation for every minute you speak).

☐ I sought to understand the goals of the event and event organizers.

☐ I have a clearly-defined problem and have given the audience a reason to care about it.

☐ I am bringing my own vulnerability into the talk or presentation.

☐ I am connecting with the audience using storytelling or sensory details.

☐ I spent time rehearsing and in front of others.

☐ I have listened to myself on recordings.

☐ I have my alarm set, my outfit picked out, my water bottle filled, my computer charged, and backup files ready to go.

And the "after checklist" might look something like this:

☐ I stuck to my talk track and didn't wander.

☐ I finished in time and got all my messages in because I practiced enough before—and watched the clock during.

☐ I didn't try to be the smartest one in the room—I brought a mindset of wanting to be helpful to them.

☐ I "listened" to the audience and adjusted my energy to keep them engaged.

(*continued*)

*(continued)*

☐ People asked questions because I got them excited to be curious about my idea.

☐ I recovered calmly if something went wrong. I was able to [breathe, drink water, take a break, use humor] to address it.

☐ I went to bed on time the night before.

☐ I brought my best self.

You might add your own statements to this checklist that lead to your success. In short, understanding how you were an effective speaker is as critical as being one.

### Strategies to Build Better Habits

In building your content:

- Investigate what your audience wants; don't always rely on the event planner or brief. Try to deeply understand their questions against your goals.

- Write out your communication goal for your talk or speech. Keep it in front of you as you prepare.

- Block out specific time to brainstorm, organize, write, outline, practice, design slides, revise, and more. Don't be surprised if it takes longer than you anticipate. Indeed, it often will.

- Arrange for a person to help give you feedback; block time on their calendar, too (see Principle #6).

In practicing:

- Use good posture, your full voice and full breath (see Principle #5).

- Try going "too big." What does that feel like? When you modulate back it might be the right size (especially if you are someone who is a soft talker or shy).

- Record yourself, listen back (see Principle #6).

In reflection after you practice or deliver:

- Write down what worked for you, note what didn't, celebrate anything that did (no matter how small).

- Pick *one thing* to improve upon next time. Even if it was perfect, we always have something new to work on.

- Look for the next opportunity to try.

We know that habits can be incredibly hard to both break and build. For inspiration and guidance on

*(continued)*

how to build sustainable habits we highly recommend two books:

*Atomic Habits*, by James Clear. This book provides a practical framework to improving bit by bit. This is exactly the kind of habitual improvement that we know leads speakers to success.[4]

*The 7 Habits of Highly Successful People*, by Steven R. Covey. This seminal business book is worth a reread as you think about creating habits around your speaking practice. The habits Covey outlines are 100% relevant.[5]

# 2

# Speaking Is Messy

There are many interpretations of "messy." We chose that word intentionally because we really, really mean it. Many trips to the thesaurus later, no word better suits this concept.

When we first developed this threshold concept, we initially called it "Speaking is a non-linear process," but that didn't truly encapsulate everything we needed to say on this topic. So we iterated. It's one of our favorite things to do, and such an important part of our process. What we realized as we iterated and tried to find a name or word that made sense for this was that in order to really capture what we meant, we had to go simple. We landed on "messy." In every way, our arrival at that word is the perfect example of this threshold concept.

Let's frame it this way: How do you approach something that is messy, like a closet, desk, or kitchen after a big family meal? Do you jump in, do you procrastinate, do you delegate or just pretend it doesn't exist? Speaking can feel messy like any of those scenarios: unwanted, uncharted, unfamiliar, but always unavoidable. This threshold will force you to encounter a lot of feelings and emotions that can make you feel "out of sorts."

Robert Frost eloquently said, "The best way out is always through."[1] And popular author on the stoics, Ryan Holliday, reminds us, "The obstacle is the way."[2]

Instead, we suggest finding clarity in the chaos. But don't let the messiness of public speaking discourage you. Embrace the chaos as a natural part of the process. From uncertainty to anxiety, it's all part of crafting a compelling talk. Even the best speakers need to navigate the mess so they can eventually deliver greatness.

Remember that TEDxColumbus speaker who took himself out of state on a silent retreat to a quiet cabin for three days? *Yes, it can take that long.* He came back with the best ten minutes of a talk. He worked through the mess, many times over.

The mess is normal, but we also know that it can cause anxiety, fear, and uncertainty. And that feels uncomfortable or just downright icky.

Embrace it and know it's just a part of the process.

Let's review the main messes you might encounter.

## Effective Public Speaking Starts With Organizing the Mess

The process of speaking usually starts with thoughts and ideas swirling around in the brain. While they might make sense to the speaker, they will require some organization for anyone else to understand. We see this happen in four primary ways:

- A few words on Post-it notes or an outline
- A transcription of a spoken "draft" into a recording or voice memo
- A full written script
- A series of questions to be answered, in order

All of these are processes that help to group, sort, edit, and decide what to say and how long to say it.

Barbara Minto, the revered author of *The Pyramid Principle*, pioneered the procedural knowledge on how to get any communicator to the highest value and concise structure of the information. She does not explain how to narrate that structure or tell a great story, but she did teach us that there can be (and should be) a hierarchy of thought that can inform what gets in and what gets left out of a communication.[3]

We know that structure also aids an audience in understanding and resonating with any message.

Consider this question we often pose: "How long would it take you to feel uncomfortable if you got in a friend's car and they started driving but didn't tell you where they were going?" Under the right circumstances, maybe you're up for an adventure. But, more than likely, you want to have some idea of what is about to happen.

That's what it's like to listen to someone talk without an underlying structure. You don't have a clue where they are going. We address specific structures in depth later in this concept.

All structures have their place and strength in developing an effective talk, but you will always have to consider what will work best for your specific content, goals, and particular audience.

We know this for sure. You'll be hard pressed to find an audience that loves the "journey story" where you start at the beginning of time and which takes you through every step, conversation, and turn. We suspect your audience will only be asking, "Where are you taking me, when will we get there, and why should I care?"

This threshold is not meant to teach the structure but to make sure a speaker encounters it in their talk development.

We have lots of ways to support speakers in doing this. Acacia shares a story about one of her favorite methods here:

---

### Acacia: Tapping Into Intuitive Structure

I have a bias. One that comes from my experience creating original theatre:

*Sometimes we lean too heavily on logic when we are working creatively.*

*Nothing against thinking. Ask anyone on the Articulation team, and they will tell you I spend a lot of time thinking—sometimes far too much time. But, I also know that intuition matters, and finding ways to move and embody your thinking in some way can show you connections that you might miss if you stay in your head.*

In 2018, I was working with a new speaker as she prepared for her TEDxColumbus talk. Like many speakers, she had been thinking about a very big idea for years before she was invited to the stage. She in fact had so many ideas she wanted to share, but in the spirit of TEDx, a very limited time to do so.

Early in our work together, we noticed that talking about those ideas, thinking about them, and writing about them wasn't getting her where she needed to go in actually structuring a talk.

So we went to one of our tried-and-true strategies. A very high-tech invention called the Post-it note.

Each idea, each story, each quote, each data point, every little thought got its own Post-it note. Before we knew it, there were notes stuck all over the wall of my tiny office.

She started to see connections. She was moving Post-it notes. Discovering themes and threads. Her message became clearer and clearer.

When she finally delivered the talk, the audience was rapt. They laughed, they were challenged, and they felt a call to action. The talk was not what she had expected when she started—it was much better.

Indeed, a study in 2002 by Margaret Wilson called "Six Views of Embodied Cognition" reinforced what happened with this speaker (and many others). By physically manipulating objects (like the Post-it notes), it helped improve thinking and problem-solving. Wilson proved that deeper processing and better understanding comes from any physical activity which helps to organize information both in the body *and* the brain.[4]

You don't have to invest in a bunch of Post-it notes to work on your own presentations. This is only one method. And only one approach. Every communication will begin with organizing the mess of thoughts and ideas in your head. How *you* begin and proceed will be uniquely yours . . . and will likely change.

## There Are Multiple Starting Points and Structures

This can feel messy to speakers who are used to a certain order of revealing information (like academic researchers— we see you). But the reality is, there is no right or wrong way to start a talk, or your process of crafting one. Here are some options:

1. "What is the one thing you want the audience to take away from your talk?" In other words, start with the conclusion.

2. What's the problem you are trying to solve? Frame that as the beginning. It is the opposite of #1 above.

3. Perhaps you start with a critical moment: "I stumbled upon this data point . . ." that sent you on a new adventure leading to this solution/idea—and talk.

4. "When I was a kid . . ." is a fine place to begin, too. Sometimes a deep memory or experience has shaped what you are about to share.

The goals of your communication, the genre you are speaking in, and the people you are speaking to might help guide you on where to start. These are not independent components; in fact, they are very interdependent.

One powerful place to start your organizational process is with a question *the audience wants you to answer*. This is especially true when presenting to executive leadership.

But it's not the only place to begin as you determine what you will share. Invited to give a keynote? Maybe you start with what you want the audience to take away. Called to welcome a group of new employees? Perhaps you begin with a story from your first days with the organization and what you wish you'd known.

No matter where you begin, you will always want to circle back to *your communication goals*; what do you want the audience to do with the information when you are done speaking?

Moving on from where to start, you'll have many choices in the structure of your talk. It is well understood that audiences can follow speakers who have *some* structure in their talk. This is in contrast to a speaker that just meanders through random thoughts without any specific question or theme. We share some common structure examples for your talk at the end of the chapter that might help you get started.

But it's important to remember that no matter which structure you choose, there are no hard-and-fast rules about how to use them. Acacia recalls a particular time when a client got a little too rigid with the structure, and how it stalled her out.

---

### Acacia: The Unlocked Door

Have you ever gotten stuck preparing a communication?

In our Message Method class, we aim to move teams and individuals toward clarity and concision in organizing their message. The final step of the workshop is a real-life application: participants take what they learned and apply it to a real-life communication they need to prepare for a near-future audience and event.

I remember a leader who came to this final application part of the workshop and expressed that she had really struggled to apply the method. She had spent a lot of time trying and banging her head against a metaphorical wall. As a facilitator, I thought, this signals a failure on behalf of me, the teacher. What had I not helped her understand?

As I listened, it quickly became clear what had gotten in her way. She had followed the process a little *too* closely.

She started with her audience and what they were hoping to hear just as we'd taught in the class. This is usually a great place to begin—if the audience has an agenda, you want to be on it. If you've ever presented and been interrupted, this is likely the issue.

But this speaker was preparing for a breakout at a conference. She didn't know exactly who would be in the room let alone what was on their minds. So she got stuck.

She needed to know that she could start at any point in the process she had just learned and work her way backward, forward, or all around. I told her, "If one door is locked, try another."

When I encouraged her to start *elsewhere*, the communication and its structure opened up.

For her, she knew exactly what idea she wanted to share. From there we worked backward, asking ourselves, "What might get the audience interested and make them want to hear her message?"

Sometimes the simple act of letting go of how you think things will go and giving yourself some grace to try again will help you break through when you're stuck.

The key lesson? Don't be afraid to lean into the mess. It may just reveal the talk you actually want to give.

There's one other consideration to keep in mind, because audiences are notoriously lacking in attention nowadays, thanks to so many distractions. We can't stress enough the need to narrate the structure. Consider yourself the tour guide of your own communication. This honestly goes back to one of the foundational components we learned early in speaking:

*Tell them what you are going to tell them, tell them, then tell them what you told them.*

Here we attempt it:

*Remember, it doesn't matter how you arrive at the structure you choose for your communication, just so long as you have one that allows the audience to follow you.*

## Working on a Talk Takes Many Iterations

For the perfectionists (and recovering perfectionists) who want to get it right the first time, this feels especially messy.

Wherever you start in the process, it may take many tries to "get it right." And there are many parts and pieces that might need work. Be patient with yourself. Your first idea may be good, but you should expect to iterate on your ideas. Don't settle. Keep thinking about your ideas and refining them. You'll know when you've gotten to the right one. Further, if visuals are needed or included, the process will take additional iteration to design and decide what they are and how they can support a talk.

This is why we are never surprised when our clients make drastic changes to content and ideas between calls. It's part of the reason we give so much time between sessions in the first place—so they can have a moment to wrestle with their own ideas and refine and come back with the idea that makes the most sense. All of us have clients who charge into the process assured they have the right talk direction, but after some time and space, really thinking about the audience and their goals, realize a narrower (or broader) idea would be better suited.

Acacia experienced an example of this not too long ago. What makes this story great is that Acacia wasn't the one giving the feedback; the client's peers guided her to a more successful outcome!

---

### Acacia: Backward Steps Can Move You Forward

I was coaching a group of speakers like any number that we coach—a small cohort of smart, rising executives tapped to give a presentation inside a large company meeting.

One of them showed up ready to go. She had done her homework to prepare for the call. Her idea was clear. Well articulated. Well organized. Easy to follow. Light years ahead of others in that respect.

For a moment, I thought it would be smooth sailing for her. But then came the questions from her peers:

What is new here?

When do I need to know this?

Who is this talk for?

*(continued)*

(*continued*)

Suddenly the idea itself was being questioned. These questions let her know that what she was saying might not be interesting enough. She was going to need to dig deeper if she wanted to really engage the audience. She faltered. I could see her visibly shrink. She honestly looked so deflated.

As a coach I wanted to comfort her and let her know it would be all right. That this was a good sign and the right moment for it to happen. That this mess was a normal part of the process. That she could trust the process, messy as it is, and that she would come out the other side. And with an even better presentation than she could imagine.

But I also knew I couldn't take away her discomfort. Nor should I. This was a threshold concept she needed to wrestle with. One that can be uncomfortable, but also transformative. So I let her sit with the discomfort and gave her a few reminders. Most notably: "We always start with a lot of ideas in our head; sometimes it takes a few rounds to find the ones that are best suited for the event, audience and goal." And also, "You can do this."

We'd like to believe that crafting a presentation can be simple, and that a seasoned communicator doesn't have to wade through the mess. We'd like to believe that you can sit down and write a speech in one go from beginning to end. But even if you know what you want to say when you sit down, it may take more than a few tries to get it right.

## Writing and Speaking Are Different Messes

All of the ideas we've shared so far surrounding this threshold concept could easily apply to writing, too—the organization of ideas, starting anywhere (as long as you put pen to paper or fingers to keyboard), iteration. These are all true for creating a written communication. So we acknowledge that writing can be messy. But there is a huge difference between a written communication and a spoken one. Let's look at why.

The practice of writing a speech or verbal presentation can be a useful thought exercise. But deliver 30 seconds of a written script to us over the phone and we'll tell you to *stop reading*. It's that easy to spot. A script can, in many cases, hinder successful speaking. Beyond being incredibly difficult to memorize, writing differs from speaking in several key ways.

One, unless you are a seasoned speechwriter, you may not understand that spoken word breath patterns are not often considered *when you write*. This is largely because people write in longer sentences (12–16 words) than they generally speak (8–10 words). Thanks to John McWhorter, the *New York Times* language columnist, and his TED talk, we were awakened to this important difference. The shorter sentences we speak allow for more breath, more pauses.[5]

But there are other differences as well, in formality, word choice, grammar, and repetition, which are indicators of editing or lack thereof. We don't have a thesaurus at the ready when we're in conversation, so we don't always pick the most perfect word over the one that comes to mind fastest. And we often use vernacular phrasing when we speak, which might be offensive to an English teacher if they were diagramming our sentences. Transitional cues (as described in Principle #5) are also far more common and occur more fluidly in speaking than in writing.

We never know how open our clients will be to trying a new approach to communications, even when they actively seek us out as coaches. While we discussed how important it is to build new habits in Principle #1, we all know that old habits are hard to break. This next story of Ruth's is a perfect example of old (writing) habits dying hard and why it can feel messy to move between writing and speaking.

---

### Ruth: A Tale of Two (Practice) Stories

A not-so-successful practice experience happened around 2010 when I was coaching an academic leader in town for a TEDx talk. In a somewhat non-traditional sequence for our coaching, he sent me his written draft, and I sent a few notes back. He sent me another draft. *Gulp*.

I knew after the second round of edits he was treating this like a writing exercise. And indeed, many people use writing to organize thoughts, concepts, themes, messages. There is nothing wrong with that.

Before he sent back a third round, I sent this note:

*"Remember, you are not allowed to read these words, they have to be delivered and spoken—without notes—and as if you are embodying these ideas."*

*"Oh . . . right," he said sheepishly. "I totally forgot the genre of a TED talk and that I couldn't read a script— not sure why!"*

He had a hard time pulling the talk into an outline and getting it to be embodied after that. But he certainly tried.

In contrast, not long after that engagement I came across a remarkable pattern of practice hearing how Janet Echelman prepared her wildly popular TED Talks.

She too worked on her outline but then recorded it—as best she could. Next, she had it transcribed (well before voice-to-text or AI was perfected) and used the transcription *to see what she had said*—not written. Then she would do it again.

Her talk was flawless—it was not scripted but fully embodied. Not memorized but elegantly performed. She reflected on her process and habits afterwards in a podcast, ones I've clearly embraced and taught to hundreds of others.

We encourage you to watch Janet Echelman's talk.[6] It's a fantastic example of what can happen when you don't write your talks. We've coached countless speakers to the same types of successes. When someone is willing to lean into this idea, it has a huge payoff. Try it for yourself and see.

# The Messiest of Them All: Speaking Always Has a Time Limit

Ruth regularly says, "In the boxing match of time versus content, time always wins."

Psychologist and Executive Function expert Russell Barkley identified time management, the ability to estimate time and use it effectively, as one of our many executive functions.[7] In speaking, this means knowing how long your talk should be, how long it was when practiced, and then while delivering it—how long you've gone, how long you have left, what you can cut on the fly—and how to wrap up gracefully when you are about to go over.

It plays out in this way:

A speaker takes the stage; they are given 30 minutes to present (regardless of the genre, just go with the story for the sake of the point).

At 28 minutes, the audience is ready for the speaker to come to a conclusion.

At 29 minutes, they start wondering if that will happen.

At 30 minutes and 30 seconds, the speaker is not done. But the audience is.

At 31 minutes, the audience gets agitated.

At 32 minutes, the audience begins to look at their phones.

At 33 minutes, the audience is gone. Physically, intellectually, emotionally, you name it.

That is messy. The speaker hasn't finished. He didn't get to a quarter of his talk. The audience doesn't care. Their contract was to be attentive for 30 minutes.

Not to mention the poor speaker who was supposed to go next who is now frantically trying to cut their presentation down to fit in the remaining time.

The limitation of time is one of the messiest parts of presenting. If a speaker had all the time in the world, they could share everything they want to share. Because they don't have unlimited time, speakers are forced to make hard decisions about what they can include. We call that part of the process "killing your darlings." It can be painful *and* messy.

In fact, we often make it even tougher by coaching our clients to a shorter length talk than what is called for. A 15-minute talk? We'll coach it to be 12–13 minutes. That way the speaker has built in time for the inevitable mess that occurs in the retelling (most speakers go longer live than they do in practice).

In complex oral interviews (set up to defend a written bid for a very large contract) that we coach, undeniably, one of the hardest phases of preparation is in the editing to time. These are high-stakes proposal defense moments. Everyone has a mountain of content they truly believe needs to be heard. But the client (or prospective client) has imposed a time limit. And like we said above, it doesn't matter how much you have to say; it only matters that you say it inside the time the client provided. We want to be clear—this doesn't give you permission to speed up to fit everything in.

We'll conclude the messy conversation with this non-rhetorical question:

*"How much information do you need to provide for someone to believe something is true?"*

Answering that, plus the rigorous use of a clock, a recording device, and maybe the careful use of an AI tool for some editing suggestions, can help you navigate the mess and get you to—or under—the time limit.

If you have any doubts about just how important staying within time is, Acacia's story about a startup team at a pitch competition will erase them completely.

---

### Acacia: Time Is a Contract

I was helping a group of entrepreneurs pitch their new startup. Their technology was impressive—potentially life-saving. As they told me more, I could see that they were solving a real problem, had a viable target market, a distinct competitive advantage, and a roadmap to profitability. In short, they had a ton of potential for the right investor.

This was the first pitch for potential investors. Real investing is not like *Shark Tank*. The goal was not to get the investor to open their checkbook that day, but instead to open the door—one that invited more conversations that would lead to significant investment.

They had eight minutes to pitch followed by seven minutes of questions. When they presented the pitch to me, it was over 12 minutes.

As I always do, I gave them the facts: they were way over time. They would have to cut content because no amount of "tightening" was going to help them drop one third of their time.

Surprisingly, this group pushed back. They argued that their total time block was 15 minutes. If they went over the eight-minute requested pitch, they would just lose time for questions. "No big deal," they told me.

I was taken aback. "Very big deal," I said.

These investors weren't simply evaluating their product, I reminded them. They were evaluating the team. Were these people they trusted?

The time they gave the team *was a contract* these investors had made with them—one of their earliest. They had asked for eight minutes of presentation and seven minutes of questions. I pointedly asked the team, "Would *you* want to do business with someone who breaks their word the first time you meet them?"

Time matters. It shows respect for the audience. If the audience wants more time with you, let them ask. But never take it without permission.

## Speaking Requires Adaptability to Drive Through the Mess of Actually Speaking

Ruth's family has a remote cabin in West Virginia. Up the road lives a hard-working family that runs a massive self-sustainable farm with a bed-and-breakfast for travelers. They hunt, they fish, they raise seven different kinds of animals,

14 different vegetables, fruits, flowers, herbs, and more. Like a well-practiced speaker, they have all of their dispositions, core skills, and habits integrated into a well-oiled system.

One day a deer sauntered onto their property, looking to use the potato field for their daily buffet. The farmer, Kendall, invited Ruth to participate in the killing and skinning of the deer, as it was wreaking havoc on their crop. Ruth, the city girl, was equally intrigued and scared to take on such a task, but went for it anyway. She walked away remembering one thing: how pissed Kendall was. A small complication evoked a lot of emotion and total distraction from the other 10 tasks on his list for the day.

At any point in the speaking process, "a deer" can walk into your talk and distract you, causing a mess and probably an emotional response that will require you to refocus on the task. Your job is not to eradicate all the emotion that will flood you, but to know how to respond and react.

Of course we don't *want* something to go wrong when we take the stage or it's our turn to speak in a meeting, but something usually does. How do we count the ways? We've heard a lot of harrowing stories. Acacia's client, Henry, had an epic experience, just one of the dozens (hundreds?) we had to choose from.

Henry is a global business leader who had been working on his presence and speaking for a while. He had just returned from one of his largest keynotes to date. On top of that, it was his first time in front of an entirely international audience in Thailand, complete with interpreters.

After the event, and knowing how important this moment was, Acacia asked, "How did your keynote go!?"

Much to her surprise, Henry laughed ruefully and replied: "Well . . . it was unexpected, I can tell you that."

He had prepared diligently. He had simplified his message. In their preparation, he stayed attuned to English idioms and removed each one so that his message was as accessible as possible. He had practiced out loud. He even had a rehearsal on the actual stage to practice and work out any technical issues.

But then "the deer" sauntered in.

The lavalier microphone mysteriously stopped working. He was handed a handheld microphone which he had never used before. He had to hold the new mic up high to his face—and click through his slides with the other hand. This was not easy for a guy who talks with his hands in a good way!

On top of that, while he had prepared his content for this international audience, he hadn't thought about what it would feel like for him to have an audience respond differently than his typical American audiences. They were quieter and more intent on listening than expressing. He found this disorienting and it left him occasionally stuck in his head.

Indeed, this is the mess of speaking. Something will, more than likely, go "wrong." Or at least not as planned. Your ability to accept that mess and keep moving forward will be what carries you through. In Henry's case, he had prepared so well, he was able to adapt and still nail his message.

If Henry's experience doesn't seem familiar to you, do any of these messy statements hit home for you?

- My notecards fell and I got them out of order and couldn't find the one with the third story . . . and I just forgot it.
- The projector was at a different ratio than my slides and all of my fonts got messed up.
- The power went out.
- The speaker before me went very long and I had to reduce my talk by half.
- My flight got canceled and I had to move my talk to another time, after a really great keynote.
- My client wanted me to cut my talk into half—so they could have lunch in the middle.
- I just blanked. I knew it 'cold' but I just couldn't recall it once I got on stage.
- I started coughing and couldn't stop. That's never happened before!

Maybe all of them?

**Adaptability** is fueled by the knowledge something will go wrong and, when it does, you can say "great, there it is!" Audiences will be patient—they are always rooting for you. But your rigor in practicing, having some backup plans and being honest in the moment will carry you through any hiccup you will face.

Jon Petz, a National Speakers Association Hall of Fame member, loves to share stories of all the things that have spontaneously gone wrong during his 20 years of being a professional speaker and emcee. From it all he shared one piece of advice with Ruth during a conversation, drawn from his days of being a magician: "Have an *out*." He says if you have a planned card trick and the wrong card gets pulled, you always have an "out" to explain or distract from the error. He takes his own advice seriously and imagines "outs" for everything from a slide deck and microphone failing to a canceled plane or lost luggage.[8]

Here's an out we love, and you may never say it but it's the right mindset trick when you are in fear of not being perfect on stage or not being able to answer all the questions in a business pitch:

"Of the 7,252 questions or scenarios we prepared for, that was not one of them. Give me a minute to figure this out." Or, "We are happy to get back to you this afternoon with an answer to that question." It always elicits a laugh and realization that being adaptable and honest in the moment can still earn you points. A little sense of humor can also break the tension and reality that despite our best attempts, we will never be perfect.

## Takeaway

Maybe you are comfortable with mess. Maybe you're learning to get comfortable with it. Either way, it is unavoidable in the world of speaking. No matter how practiced or masterful you are, this threshold concept will sneak up on you in often unwelcome ways.

In practice, this can make becoming a better speaker feel a little like a game of whack-a-mole. As soon as you think you've figured things out, the ground will shift and you will have to change things. When you can point to it, and learn to say "Yep, there the mess is again," you might learn to enjoy this aspect of speaking.

## Best Practices for Messy

Our mantra for messy:

**"Work through the mess, not around it."**

Our own practice and storytelling coaching pulls on several fundamental writings such as Barbara Minto's *The Pyramid Principle* (how to get to the highest value message), Annette Simmons' *The Story Factor* (what is a story and why do they work?),[9] and Paul Smith's *Lead with a Story* (when stories are best used),[10] not to mention a lot of common sense about how listeners seek meaning and understanding, in general.

### Bring Order to the Mess With Structure

Here are some of our favorite narrative structures that help calm the chaos of anyone with too much content in too little time.

1. What, So What, Now What

   This structure is excellent for presenting a clear and actionable message.

   • **What:** Start by clearly stating the topic or issue you're addressing. Present the facts, data, or observations that define the "What."

- **So What:** Explain the significance of the "What." Why should the audience care? What are the implications or consequences?
- **Now What:** Conclude with a call to action or proposed solution. What steps can be taken to address the issue or capitalize on the opportunity?

Example:

- **What:** Climate change is causing rising sea levels.
- **So What:** This threatens coastal communities and infrastructure.
- **Now What:** We must invest in renewable energy and sustainable infrastructure.

2. Problem, Solution, Benefit

This structure is ideal for persuasive presentations where you're advocating for a specific solution.

- **Problem:** Clearly define the problem or challenge. Highlight its impact and urgency.
- **Solution:** Present your proposed solution. Explain how it addresses the problem effectively.
- **Benefit:** Emphasize the positive outcomes or advantages of implementing your solution.

*(continued)*

(*continued*)

Example:

- **Problem:** Traffic congestion is increasing in our city, wasting time and fuel.
- **Solution:** We could implement a smart traffic management system.
- **Benefit:** This would reduce commute times, improve air quality, and increase productivity.

3. Cause, Effect, Impact

This structure is useful for explaining a phenomenon or event and its consequences.

- **Cause:** Identify the root cause or trigger of the situation.
- **Effect:** Describe the direct and indirect consequences or outcomes.
- **Impact:** Analyze the broader implications or long-term effects.

Example:

- **Cause:** Deforestation is increasing rapidly.
- **Effect:** The result is biodiversity loss and habitat destruction.
- **Impact:** Which ultimately disrupts our ecosystems and accelerates the effects of climate change.

4. Past, Present, Future State

This structure is effective for showcasing progress, setting goals, or presenting a vision.

- **Past:** Briefly review the historical context or previous state of affairs.

- **Present:** Describe the current situation, challenges, and opportunities.

- **Future:** Outline your vision for the future or desired outcomes.

Example:

- **Past:** Limited access to education in rural areas is a problem that goes back generations.

- **Present:** Technology and distance learning bring a new potential for increased enrollment in rural areas.

- **Future:** We now have the power to truly allow for universal access to quality education for all.

5. Context, Action, Result

This structure is great for quickly telling a story.

- **Context:** Share the time, place and characters of the story along with what the main character wants.

*(continued)*

(*continued*)

- **Action:** Describe what actually happened.
- **Result:** Conclude the story with a call to action or next step.

Example:

- **Context:** Ten years ago, two Midwesterners decided to take their first trip out west.
- **Action:** They saw mountains for the first time and were awed.
- **Result:** And decided to go back every year.

### Grounding for Emotional Moments

Speaking can be difficult, especially if emotion is involved. This can range from communicating a difficult *decision* (layoffs, budget cuts), to sharing a difficult *situation* (tragic or traumatic life event), to something that is just very "touchy" thanks to a challenging relationship or company politics (not even mentioning national politics, which for sure has caused more emotions than ever before).

Additionally, in specific communication moments, you might find yourself frustrated by a virtual audience who won't turn on their cameras and don't engage. A colleague might ask a question that throws you and your work under the bus.

You will need to be able to rein in your emotional response to continue to communicate effectively. You will need to be able to stay grounded and not allow that frustration to throw you off.

While we don't encourage it, we have worked with many speakers who are still in active stages of grief—while they are trying to speak about it. Think: a domestic abuse situation, the loss of a loved one, someone formerly human trafficked, a survivor of a devastating disease. In these cases, we tell speakers it's okay to cry, but you want to be ready to stop crying and keep going. Your audience never minds you feeling something, but they also need you to be able to re-center yourself and carry on.

Here are our favorite strategies to work through these moments:

- Visiting and practicing in the room before you speak is the best first defense. Most of the anxiety goes away when you can see where you will be looking, where the audience is sitting, where to see your slides and more.

- Mingling with an audience before you speak is golden. You get to see your audience one-on-one as people and their interactions will help you feel supported.

*(continued)*

(*continued*)

- Record yourself and hear your version of the story. Hearing it will give you confidence.

- Reduce the amount of detail you will give for the story, as to not evoke too many visual memories for yourself.

- Imagine your feet have roots, deeply woven into the earth. Let the earth be a place to find literal grounding. It will not come out from under you, even in moments when you feel like you are in a free-fall.

- If you know there are delicate or tender moments that may make you choke up, have a keyword that can help you trigger out of it. Often, that word can help begin the story you are to tell right after.

For more on emotional grounding visit the Core Skills section later in the book.

### Strategies to Navigate the Mess

- If you love processes or have perfectionist tendencies, know that this will be a difficult threshold for you.

- Leave time for rounds of iteration. The more important the communication, the more iteration you should expect and the more you should involve others.

- Do your first-draft, high-level outline quickly (like within an hour). Know it is a *first step* which can help set the stage for proof, details, and revisions. Do not try to be perfect at the start.

- Eventually identify a structure that works best for the communication you need/want to give. You may not know what it is at the beginning, but your audience will want to hear it when you deliver it.

- Resist writing a script. Instead, consider recording yourself and transcribe from that attempt. You'll be surprised how much easier it is than trying to put pen to paper.

- However, do write out the first and last sentence of any presentation—"getting in" and "getting out" are always the hardest parts of speaking.

- Consider using AI tools in limited ways to help narrow down content. Prompts like, "How can I say this in half the time" or "Put this text into something conversational" can get you more quickly to time limits and narrative styles that audiences expect. (Pro tip: if you ask it to remove content, on the next prompt, ask it "what content was removed," so you don't have to compare versions.)

- When you're given a time limit, plan to speak for fewer minutes than you've been asked to. Your talk will expand in real time.

# 3

# Speaking Is Social

Of course speaking is social. Unless, well, you talk to yourself. You never do that, right?

An idea starts in your head, and it must wind its way through your thoughts and memories, through the language centers in your brain, and finally into your breath and vocal cords and tongue and teeth, into the air where the vibrations finally make their way to the ears of a listener, your audience. That sound then goes into their ears and through their own language processing centers as they interpret your words through their own understanding and memories. This is what makes speaking social. The complex interaction of two brains separated by space and time.

The truth that all speaking is social explores the academic definition of influence (rhetoric), how it is risky, temporal and involves listening.

It sounds very academic to use the word *rhetoric*. But no other word in the English language exists that means the same: *the art of effective or persuasive speaking or writing*.

We persuade and affect people through the use of *logos, pathos,* and *ethos. Logos* appeals to a person's logic and reason; it is the beauty of a well-structured argument. *Pathos* helps us remember to take the emotions and values of the audience into consideration, inviting them to feel something. Finally, there is the role of the communicator themself; whether we trust their credibility is where *ethos* comes into play.

These three pillars of rhetoric are ultimately about moving an audience to do something.

That brings us back to the question that started our threshold concept journey. (It is not lost on us that it is indeed a "rhetorical one.")

*"When was the last time you said something in general to no one in particular?"*

Self-talk (before or after coffee) doesn't count.

Just like we don't write without a purpose or audience, we don't speak without a purpose or audience.

For example, when you wake up, you ask your child to pick up her room; she is your audience. Your goal is to inspire her to find the floor. And relocate the wet towel that is causing mold in your carpet.

You then get to work and have to share a report that shows a downward trend in a supply chain issue, to your peer who is your audience. Your purpose is to alert them about the potential threat to the manufacturing timeline upon which the holiday season sales are dependent so that they can decide whether or not to do something about it.

At the end of the day, you attend a PTA meeting at your child's school. You raise your hand to attempt to share an idea about the upcoming fundraiser. Your audience may be the board or other parents, but the purpose is ultimately to try to raise more funds.

When you speak with purpose, you are trying to move an audience to some action, which makes it inherently rhetorical.

Whether it's a full theater of 1,000 colleagues or your child at home, that audience is undeniably part of the *meaning-making process.*

You can say one thing and think it is clear, but the meaning is made in the mind of the listener.

Pollster Frank Luntz has cemented our thinking: "It's not what you say. It's what people hear."[1]

Moreover, audiences today have never been more distracted by any number of technology tools and social media channels causing truly diminishing attention spans.

And for those who work in a laboratory, this is a heavier lift. By the way, we consider any space where you work in a tight-knit group of peers deep inside an expert space a lab. It might be scientifically based but it may be technology, manufacturing, or any other space that requires deep subject matter expertise that can lead to discovery and solving problems. Or it may be the back office of a major league baseball team run by Billy Beane (the real-life protagonist of *Moneyball*) analyzing stats from last night's game.

The language you use inside your science or industry is not often easily understandable outside it. The minute you step outside your lab to speak to a lay audience, (again) it isn't what you say, it's what they hear. And if you use concepts, language, and acronyms they don't understand, they won't hear anything.

## Speaking Moves an Audience Toward a Goal

Imagine you are invited to speak to a specific audience at a designated time and place.

The first question you must always ask yourself: What is my communication goal? Or, what do I want the audience *to do* when I am done talking?

In their threshold concepts for writing, Wardle, et al. in *Naming What We Know* most clearly assert that "writing mitigates activity."[2] This is also true in speaking.

We rarely, if ever, speak just to speak. There is some goal to your speaking.

As a speaker, your goals should be articulated more purposefully . . .

Like this:

- What do you want the audience to know (or learn)? For many speakers this is easy to define. The information

they want to share is clear in their mind. They might
need to narrow it down, or organize it, but the information is what they focus on.

- What do you want the audience to feel? This is, without doubt, the most overlooked part of articulating a
goal. Perhaps it is because our culture discourages the
discussion of emotion at work. However, humans are
emotional creatures. They make decisions not just on
information, but on feelings. Which makes them an
essential part of any speaking goal.

- What do you want the audience to do? Ultimately, we
speak in order to move a person to action. Especially
in business. When a speaker is unclear about what they
want the audience to do, listeners are left wondering,
"Why am I here?"

Another way of looking at your goal is to think about
what question you are answering for your audience.

In our workshops we have an exercise where we ask participants to answer a question phrased exactly this way:

*How do you get bread?*

We don't define "get." We leave it to the listener's
imagination. Some will start with going to the bank to get
money. Others might jump in with ingredients like flour
and water. Still others will start with going to the field to
harvest some wheat. The question is simply too broad to
be useful.

We work tirelessly to help speakers best define the question they are answering. *Narrow the question to the right size.*

In our exercise, that iteration may look like:

*How do we get bread?*
*How do we find bread we like at the store?*
*How do we find bread to buy for a gluten-sensitive family member within a 10-mile radius of our home the day before Thanksgiving?*

Or . . .

*How do we get bread?*
*How do we find the ingredients to make bread?*
*How do we find the ingredients to make bread for a gluten-sensitive family member?*

And then you have to think about the audience. Sometimes they will need a lot of context. Other times, it is the question you need to answer for a specific person who needs very little.

Clarity in what you want your audience to know, feel or do is a necessary threshold toward learning to be a great communicator.

In our experience, the part that most surprises people is the "feel." Many speakers are not considering how they want their audience to feel. But what's the point in giving a talk at all if you aren't clear about what you want your audience to *do*. Blythe had an eye-opening experience with a very famous speaker who left that part of the talk out entirely.

## Blythe: Move Me to Action Please

When *Hillbilly Elegy* came out, I read it, because I (a) live in Ohio and was curious about Vance's experience living in Ohio, (b) drove through and visited the parts of the state Vance spoke about for work, and (c) had the opportunity to hear JD Vance speak, and I wanted to attend prepared. This was before he became a politician, at a time when he was vehemently saying that he wasn't interested in being a politician. Don't worry, this story is not about his politics; it's about his speaking.

I don't remember all the details of the talk. He was . . . fine. I do remember how I felt at the end, though. I was left a little unsatisfied.

He shared moments from his own personal story, talked about how amazing (and at times, uncomfortable) it was to go to Yale Law School after getting an undergraduate degree from Ohio State. He impressed us with the importance of lifting bright, accomplished individuals from backgrounds and situations like his into new, more aspirational opportunities. He also pointed out that those individuals can get caught between two disparate places, and never really feel like they fit in either.

And there we were. A roomful of people with deep pockets with nothing to do. He hadn't recommended the next step. No call to action.

*(continued)*

(*continued*)

I left thinking, "*What did he want us to do?*" It was completely dispiriting.

At the end of every talk, I want, and we all want, to be moved to some action. Even if it is believing, trusting or knowing. Sometimes it is investing, leveraging or in Vance's future talks—voting.

This threshold reminds speakers that one of your first tasks is to define the action you want your audience to take. It will help refine and organize your talk and, assuredly, give you a stronger ending than none at all.

## Communicating Verbally Is Inherently Risky

We don't get to be with many of our clients when they're about to go on stage to do their talks or to present at that board meeting. Our job is to give them all the preparation they need, so they feel good, ready, and confident. But we've been backstage in the big theater or at the table of a small meeting many times and have felt their anxiety and uncertainty before they speak.

No matter how confident they feel, no matter how prepared they are, nearly every single one looks like the people you see on *America's Got Talent*, hanging in the wings. They have nervous energy and are bouncy, pacing. Or they look very poised, trying to stand still, but their heart is racing. They may not even be fearful of speaking. But their body knows they are doing something difficult and risky.

That's right, speaking—communication in general, really—can be risky. We know this inherently, but why?

Why does the person who presents all the time in high-stakes situations suddenly have to go to the bathroom when she's called to present next in a low-stakes situation? Or why does the otherwise confident businesswoman prefer to hang in the background at company events?

Because there is always the *possibility of being misunderstood*. Your joke might not land. Your message might not be heard or might not be important to your audience.

If this is true, why bother with any preparation at all?

Consider your preparation to be risk mitigation. Any preparation you do, any iteration you do, any consideration of the audience helps reduce that inherent risk. And it's worth it.

Ruth works with a client in high-stakes presentations for large business bids. Her entire focus? To aggressively identify all of the potential risks to not winning and mitigate each one of them at a time—from the speaker's preparedness, to the font size on the slides, to the handoffs between speakers, to the "live demo" failure possibilities, to the most important one: Did they actually answer the question posed? And how did the client hear it?

Let's remember a classic story of a "casual comment" on an investor call. Always a high-stakes situation.

A reporter asks a question and the speaker, the corporate CEO, replies:

*"Excuse me. Next. Boring, bonehead questions are not cool. Next?"*[3]

Anyone remember this? It was 2018 and Elon Musk didn't like the question from an analyst on an investor call. It showed several layers of disrespect but ultimately was interpreted that he was being evasive about key financial matters and signaled uncertainty about Tesla's future.

Tesla's stock price fell 5% in after-hours trading that same day.

That's what we mean about risky.

Another example in the media is the "hot mic" moment, when the person wearing the mic thinks it's on mute only to learn that it isn't, and a private conversation is made humiliatingly public. You can probably recall some of these. Public figures say things that end campaigns, bring them under intense scrutiny, or get them canceled.

In 2020, Fox Sports commentator and voice of the Cincinnati Reds (and son of famed Cincinnati Reds radio commentator Marty Brennaman) Thom Brennaman used a homophobic slur over a hot mic during a game. He thought he wasn't on air at the time. But anyone watching the game heard him say it and there was no way he could deny it. Despite his profuse apology right after it happened, which he interrupted to announce a homerun, he was suspended and then stepped down from the job. Sadly, a career-ending slur.[4]

But we're not all speaking in these sorts of public environments. Let's look at how risk can impact everyday speakers.

One, a mid-level health-care executive, told Ruth that despite her total preparedness for any public speaking moment, she felt a great deal of risk. So much that her whole body felt a stress response: sweaty palms, heart racing, dry mouth, neck blotching. It only took a few minutes to reveal she had a need for control, based on a lifelong practice of being a perfectionist. It didn't help that she was in a new position, despite the fact she was wildly qualified. All of this is in contrast to what a speaker needs to be successful in the face of uncertainty: the ability to be grounded, be present and accept that something may—or will—go wrong.

Another, a senior manager at an elite beauty brand, Blythe worked with almost exclusively over Zoom. She had poise, presence, and managed her communications well, learning quickly and executing her lessons easily. When Blythe met her in person, she copped to having a really challenging time with the other part of her job—showing up and speaking at influencer events, where she felt "exposed." She said she would stumble over her words and preferred to hide in a corner—so what was the difference? Safe at her desk, in front of her computer, she considered herself protected by the distance created over video calls.

Conversely, she genuinely felt and anticipated the risks when she was standing in front of an audience. Since she was able to share this revelation, Blythe and she had an opportunity to work through the differences and ensure that she felt even more prepared for those in-person speaking moments so that she could find confidence, if not comfort, in front of a crowd.

In contrast, Acacia was working with a speaker who expressed how difficult it was to present virtually. This guy thrived in person. He knew how to read facial expressions and body language to adjust his style and content in small ways to keep the audience engaged. As he shifted to rooms filled with little black boxes with name plates, but very few faces, he had no idea how to tell if he was connecting with the audience. For the first time, he truly felt the risk of speaking, because he had no idea if the audience was understanding him.

As you can see, the impact of the risk of speaking can be felt in myriad ways.

Here's a roundup on the risks we mitigate every day in helping speakers prepare:

Risk is putting people to sleep by speaking too long or being boring. Nothing gets heard or remembered.

Risk is not understanding the balance of data and story. Too much of either will lose an audience.

Risk is speaking over your audience's head, making them feel stupid.

Risk is not defining what's at stake for your audience in listening to you. They don't see the WIFM (what's in it for me).

Risk is not practicing for any size talk, speech or presentation. Winging it rarely works out.

Risk is not paying attention to the clock, especially when audiences believe there is a time limit. They will stop listening when your time is up, even if you aren't finished.

Risk is ignoring what the host asked you to do. You won't get invited back! (Think of a panelist who says whatever they want regardless of what the moderator asks.)

Risk is reading slides. *No one* wants to be read to.

Risk is repeating yourself at the end. Audiences want you to tie your comments in an elegant ribbon.

Risk is trying to shove 100 pounds of content into a ten-pound bag. You end up racing through the messages and losing the audience along the way.

## Words Fade

Once something is said, it is gone. This is different from the risks above; it is more about understanding how an audience listens.

Let's review a few truths:

Nothing permanent remains of the words themselves once they are spoken.

The only thing that remains is the *impact* of those words.

Even in the case when public speaking is recorded, that recording cannot capture the mood and energy that exists in the room. That part of the meaning-making is actually *remade* when the video is watched later. And spliced up for social channels.

When you are reading a book, you can pause. Reread a line. Google a definition. Search for a related article. Get distracted and find a video.

But when you are listening to someone speak *live*, there is only that moment to grasp the word, the context, and the understanding.

Meanwhile, our minds are littered with thoughts, ideas, connections, and dreaming about dinner.

No wonder it's hard to listen.

We remind speakers what they say is fleeting or temporal. We also remind them that, in the words of François Fénelon, a 17th century theologian, "The more you say, the less people remember."

Working memory, or the part of short-term memory that is concerned with immediate conscious perceptual and linguistic processing, plays a role in this. It refers to the active mental process where we temporarily hold and manipulate information to perform tasks. It's like a mental work studio where you juggle multiple pieces of information to solve problems, complete tasks and make decisions. Those with ADHD often have poor working memory. Remembering what they heard and connecting it with existing knowledge can be a challenge. You can't depend on your audience to remember every word you say.

Bottom line: audiences are not perfect listeners. As much as speakers imagine they are.

It's why that old adage we shared in the last chapter bears repeating here: "Tell them what you are going to tell them, tell them, then tell them what you told them."

Assuredly the navigation of an idea will be stickier and have a greater chance of survival with those cues—especially for those who may be physically present in the audience but psychologically somewhere else.

Anything you can do to promote the stickiness of your message will make a difference. Because how frustrating is it when you repeat yourself five or six times and see no different outcome? Anyone who's a parent knows how that feels. But when you're a leader of a major corporation and your thoughts, ideas, and asks are falling on deaf ears, well, it's time to change your approach.

Acacia was sitting at an event for a client where 75 or so talented employees in succession were presenting research on opportunities in the organization. They had been asked to spend time understanding the problems they faced as a company, and coming up with a potential solution for the company. Think engagement issues, properly utilizing data, and cross-departmental collaboration.

After the groups shared their findings and clearly outlined the issues facing the organization, their leader kept getting up to talk about what they had already been doing to address the issues. He wanted them to know that they were aware and working on it.

After the fourth or fifth time he stood up, you could see that he was frustrated and confused. He said, "I thought we had talked about these things with everyone." He himself had personally shared the initiatives on town hall calls. His communications teams had shown him their messaging strategies. How was it that his team had missed the message?

Had the employees simply not been listening? Maybe. But we doubt it. The people in the room were among the most engaged employees, so it's hard to believe that they hadn't been listening.

Had he and his communication team not actually shared the information? Unlikely. In fact, they had a paper trail and video evidence to prove they had talked about each initiative.

So what was really happening?

Now, we weren't at the town halls to diagnose the issue, nor had we read the written communications being sent by the comms team. But our gut response tells us that this was an example of the temporal nature of speaking—the words simply faded.

If we had been working directly with this leader, we might have asked *how* he was sharing the message and if he was planning for this threshold concept. Was he using techniques that increase the stickiness of words? How could he use vivid storytelling to enhance recall? When and where could he repeat the message? How could he structure the communication and use headlines to help people remember?

It's easy to presume that if you say something, and think you're understood, it will also be remembered. But we all know that is simply not the case. To make your words stick, you must address the temporal nature of speaking and incorporate it into your practice.

## On Silence

In 1976, Paul Goodman unpacked in his seminal book, *Speaking and Language* that there are many kinds of silence. They are worth revisiting:

Dumb silence which accompanies slumber or apathy;

Sober silence of obligated listening;

Fertile silence of awareness, pasturing the soul, emerging new thoughts;

Alive silence of alert perception;

Musical silence that accompanies absorbed activity;

Noisy silence of resentment and self-recrimination;
Baffled silence of confusion;
The silence of peaceful accord with other persons or communion with the cosmos;
. . . and the silence of listening to another speak, catching the drift and helping him to be clear.[5]
But managing silence *while* speaking is tricky. Very tricky.

We deeply understand that a slice of silence can bring a torrent of anxiety for a speaker, but in contrast, silence can offer a cascade of clarity for their audience.

Here's where we see speakers struggle with silence—do you see yourself in any of these statements?

- I hate speaking so I want to finish quickly.
- I think that if there is a moment of silence, someone will interrupt me.
- If I don't keep talking, they will look at their phones and get distracted.
- The person who talks the most, wins.
- I don't understand (yet) where I may include pauses.
- I always prepare too much so I have to rush to fit it all in.
- I listen to all my audio podcasts and books at 1.5 speed—I've conditioned myself to speak as I've been listening.

The reason we can listen to podcasts at 1.5 speed and still understand what they're saying is that the engineer builds in pauses. When you pause for three seconds, an audience has a chance to catch up with what you've said. Some speakers think it is an invitation to be interrupted and won't take it.

In practice, pausing is complex since it is the intersection of comfort with silence and a practiced awareness of breath inside your speech pattern. But if you never pause, the ideas and words can crash together like a ten-car pileup. Emphasis to your most important words and ideas comes before and after the pause. If the pause doesn't exist, often the message will get run over on the way to that crash.

## Listen . . . While Speaking

Julian Treasure, a popular author and sound and communication expert, gave us this incredibly sticky idea: "Speak to the listening."[6] Essentially it means that as you speak, you need to keep one eye (and ear) on the audience. You must consider and note how they will *hear* your ideas. You can observe their body language, facial expressions to gauge, are they with you? Should you stop and ask, "Am I answering what questions are important today?" And if one person seems lost, confused, or disengaged, your job is to determine if it is critical that they are with you.

Yes, this is all while you are speaking. You need to listen to your audience in real time, and reflect their needs and energy in your talk. In other words, read the room. *And also respond to it.*

While listening in general has many more levels, we have defined three that work best in this application:

**Ignoring:** Speaking without considering you have an audience. At this level, you are deep in your own thoughts and ideas, perhaps your own stress response, and likely alienating your audience.

**Attempting:** You have a desire to pay attention to your audience but you aren't practiced enough and/or your nerves are in the driver's seat. This means you may lose focus to "include" the audience in your delivery, but once you hit a certain stride, it will become easier to engage and respond.

**Fully Active:** You are speaking while actively listening to and watching the audience for their feedback. You may adjust your talk to respond to their facial or body expressions of discontent or even enjoyment.

Of our vast collection of stories, the next one might be the most famous, and certainly the most often shared. It speaks loudly to a lack of listening while speaking.

---

### Ruth: Million Dollar Smile, Billion Dollar Pitch

When I started Articulation, I got a 911 call from one of my first large-company clients. I still remember it like it was yesterday:

*"One of our associates was delivering a pitch to a billion-dollar client, one of our largest ever. In the middle of it, her boss, the VP, tapped her to sit down. She wasn't done with her presentation, but she totally missed how annoyed the executives were. Apparently, she wasn't answering their questions and also didn't notice that they were grimacing, whispering to each other, and showing visible signs of discontent. She threw up on the way home on the private plane and didn't come to work today. Can you help?"*

*(continued)*

(*continued*)

After some conversations we learned this rising executive had been a teen beauty queen and was conditioned to look *between* people, not *at* them. This means that she would literally not look at the audience's faces, but rather the spaces between where they were sitting. The strategy was meant to prevent her from becoming emotional in the moment or getting distracted by seeing a smile or a disgruntled face. During this high-stakes presentation, her nervous system and stress response took the driver's seat. And lastly, it was like a "stone soup" of a presentation (throwing everything but the kitchen sink into a pot). As she tried to please everyone in assembling the deck, she pleased no one.

No wonder she couldn't *speak to the listening*. Her head was full of unhelpful behaviors, stress responses, and everyone else's words.

Speaking to the listening is a multi-sensory experience, undoubtedly. You need to be grounded in your own words, goals, and what the audience expects. Then you must be willing to "pivot" in the event that something goes, well, not according to plan.

That never happens, right? You've never been interrupted on slide 3 of a 20-page deck? Are you that person who has a "perfect" audience without thoughts and questions all along that they keep to themselves?

We'd like to meet that audience!

---

**Takeaway**

This threshold concept can be troublesome for many people. It forces you to reckon with the fact that audiences don't have to listen to you at all. You must give them a reason to, and make them the center of your message and attention.

This leads us to the character you play when you speak. YOU are not the hero of the story. Each one of your audiences is a hero. When considered in this light, speaking can become an act of generosity. One where you gift the audience something that they will be grateful for.

# Best Practices for Social

Our favorite mantra for social:

**"It's not about you."**

In other words, be as empathetic to your audience as possible. They are the hero of their own story and they will not listen to your content until you have listened to their hearts. And when you feel anxious, it might just be because you are making it about yourself—not about them.

## Want To Be Heard

While speaking has many drivers, the first one is your desire to be heard, or, to "own the room." Of course you want to, but how do you get your mindset into the space that, when you are in that room with your audience, you actually can do it?

Here are three simple exercises you can use to help gain confidence so you can show up fully present and wanting to be heard:

1. AS YOU PREPARE: Before you enter any room, *know why you want to speak* and who is giving you license to speak. This internal work gives your speaking purpose and grounding.

2. IN YOUR PRACTICE: *Try visualizing the audience responding to you.* Imagine them engaging with you,

learning, responding, maybe even getting fired up. This can help increase your excitement rather than your anxiety.

3. AT THE EVENT: Show up to the room where you are speaking the day before and practice with the actual technology set up. We assure you that 50% of your anxiety will get channeled into the ownership of your content and the audience's experience. (See Principle #5 for related suggestions.)

### Strategies for Great Audience Engagement

- Be explicit in what you want your audience to learn, feel, and do *after your communication.*
- Define the exact question you are answering for your audience, and craft the answer with them as a central character.
- Review your content and imagine someone who doesn't understand your field in the audience. Be sure you build context and define terms for them.
- Avoid the use of acronyms whenever possible, even with audiences that do understand them.
- Leave time to fit in spontaneous questions. Or better yet, plan in some key moments of interaction. Sometimes you have so much content there isn't room to look up or address a concern along the way.

*(continued)*

(*continued*)

- If you do get a spontaneous question, consider if it's a question for the whole audience. Have the fortitude to "table" questions or return to them later if they are for just one person.

- The day of your presentation, ask yourself: What does the audience need today that they may not have needed yesterday? How can you be present with them?

- Ask friends or colleagues to be a sample audience. Give the talk to them, but make sure they understand who your final audience will be (if not them). (More on this in Principle #6.)

- If you can't get humans to practice with you, try using an AI tool to analyze your audio recording. It can tell you what key points it heard. (More on AI in Your Speaking Toolkit.)

# 4

# Speaking Contains Multiple Genres

I n June 2024, Joe Biden debated Donald Trump. And then . . .

Joe Biden spoke at the rally the day after the debate, saying, "I don't debate like I used to," as he read from a teleprompter.[1]

Joe Biden was at a microphone behind a podium both times, talking about why he should retain the Presidency. But the audiences and "genres" were markedly different. And so was his performance.

A motivational speech, a board presentation, a panel discussion, a television interview, an industry conference.

Indeed, all are situations where speaking takes place. But they are all unique genres with nuances that a speaker must seek to understand.

We believe a genre is defined by at least four things: the host of the event, the goal of the event, the audience to whom you'll be speaking, and also the venue in which the event is held.

While the huge assembly of oncologists each June in Chicago might define their genre as a scientific, academic congress, the workshops, panels, and lectures within it all have slightly different goals and setups. In contrast, an investigator meeting for a clinical trial within pharmaceutical companies has one specific goal: to convey information from the primary researchers to the larger company so that others may recruit patients to test new drugs. The genre is dictated by the goal.

A recent client call reminds us that speakers (and bosses) need to pause to think about these components before making any judgments about a speaker's performance:

> *"Hey Ruth, I have an exec who just crushed a panel last week at an industry conference. But we just got home from a big pitch yesterday where he couldn't have sucked more. What do you think happened?"*

Genres. That's what happened. Let's break them down.

## A Genre Has Multiple Parts and Norms

Every genre has its own rules and conventions that affect how the audience is prepared to listen. The host of the event or meeting, an event planner, the moderator of a panel, the technology used, and the audience define these rules and norms. It should include the event structure, time constraints, room setup, delivery style (interview v. keynote, etc.) and visual style (i.e. slides) that will govern the event.

It is your job as a speaker to rigorously investigate the genre for the event or meeting at which you will be speaking. You may not always ask these questions to the organizer or leader, but as you assemble the information about the event, make sure you can answer them yourself. They will help you get closer to the expected genre.

We do, in fact, practice what we preach when we deliver keynotes and workshops at conferences and internal team meetings. So we thought we'd share how we work to identify the exact genre of the event before we show up.

We like to start with two insightful questions from Priya Parker's wonderful book, *The Art of Gathering*. She first asks, "What is the purpose for the event or meeting?" And then, "What does the audience need?" These questions allow us to understand the bigger picture of the event.[2]

Then we dig deeper and ask, "What did the event or meeting host promise the audience?" Or at least, "What did they tell them about what we will be speaking on?" These questions can help us to illuminate what the audience is expecting. Sometimes the only thing that has been shared with the audience is a title or a topic. In this case, we often recommend priming the audience ahead of time by giving them a little more insight into what to expect. But if that is not possible, we're sure to ask who is introducing us so that we can recruit them to set us up for success by giving the audience a hint at where we will be taking them in our talk.

Then we get into logistics. We want to know how much time we have to speak, if there will be a Q&A, and what is happening immediately before or after we speak. This can tell us a lot about how the audience will be listening to us.

And you can't forget about the venue. Will the audience be at round tables where they can interact easily with each other or will they be in a theater style where they expect a bit more of a performance on the stage? And of course we want to understand the technology, from how the slides will be projected, to whether there is a confidence monitor, to what type of microphone we will use.

Once we are grounded in the purpose of the event, the audience expectations, and the logistics, we revisit our goal: what we want the audience to know, feel, or do. Is it appropriate for the genre of the meeting or event? Sometimes we have the right goals for audiences but need to adjust the content for the timing. Like . . . the audience was primed for our talk but we're the last speaker after seven hours and they will really struggle to pay attention as they think about dinner. In that case, we might pivot to include more interactivity to bring the energy up.

Net-net: We make no assumptions. Or as few as possible. We invite you to do the same.

Once you have gathered all this data, you can integrate it into your preparation plan, from how you structure your content, to which examples and stories you bring, to the visual style you choose, to what you might choose to wear. It doesn't take that much effort, and knowing the answers to these questions can go a long way to mitigating risk (see Principle #3). We've provided a comprehensive list of genres at the end of this chapter to help you identify just how many there are. We urge you to avoid making assumptions about the one you are speaking to like in this next story from Ruth.

---

### Ruth: Sitting Habits and a Senior Project

At the end of his high school senior project, my son had to present reflections in front of a panel of teachers. He went into the room, sat down, shared what he'd learned and then left. It was the final step in his post-secondary journey. All that was left was graduation, literally three days later.

But the day after the panel discussion, he got an email telling him he needed to come back and try it again. He racked his brain for two days trying to imagine what he had done wrong.

The issue? Well, one was that it was unclear that he read the book they suggested. He did, but the message got a little lost. And the second? His posture.

He had spent the better part of high school sitting in odd positions due to the hyperextension in his joints. Let's just say it was one of his signature characteristics. So why would this be any different?

Well, the visual of his "slouching" was apparently far removed from their expectation of a "formal

*(continued)*

---

*(continued)*

discussion." Enough to call him in for a do-over. One teacher may have likened it to "PhD defense," which felt a little extreme, but it certainly was not a senior-lounge-kick-back-with-besties, either. Lucky for him, his second attempt was successful and checked off the absolute last box on the list to be able to graduate a few days later.

Lesson learned: ask more questions before you enter any room. And on the side of the teachers—correct the mistake in the first minute of the presentation, or state the intention *before* the student sits down.

For the rest of us, ask the appropriate questions so you have a strong sense of the genre in order to prepare properly.

## A New Genre Will Require Study and Iteration

We spent 10 years helping people understand the genre of a TED-like talk.

We coached a professor recently as he was preparing to speak to an audience of potential community partners. He shared that in creating a TED-like talk, he was breaking *all* the rules of an academic talk. It made him uncomfortable to be stepping outside of his most-practiced genre, but he was grateful to have the coaching to help guide him.

Your success in a new genre depends on your understanding of the rules and norms of that genre and *your willingness to adapt to it*. While you can blend your personal style with the style of a different genre, there can be risks involved if you do not fully understand the genre you are invited to speak in.

And shifting genres requires time. PhD candidates practice for months for their dissertation defenses; to testify to Congress takes days of practice; to prepare an oral defense for a lawsuit may take weeks or months. Be patient with yourself as you learn and understand new genres. But also, push yourself to resist falling back into familiar patterns and behaviors. In the following story, Blythe helped her client identify that this is what she was doing.

---

## Blythe: Appropriate Communication Matters

At the end of 2023, I was working with a quality assurance specialist, Annie. As we were wrapping up our coaching, she asked me what feedback I'd give her overall on her presentation skills. I had already given her feedback specific to the presentations she had done for me. From a broader perspective, I observed that she perhaps relied too heavily on written notes and I told her she could bring more of herself to her presentations and trust her knowledge.

*(continued)*

(*continued*)

(This is something I say to people often. There are lots of people who believe that they have to put on a presentation "persona." I don't recommend it. Engage authentically!)

Annie was surprised by my suggestion. She said, "I would always read my notes in university presentations, practically writing a script." That's not great, but it's also not the point of this story (see Principle #2). I'll just say that what Annie was doing for her university presentations as an aquatic biology researcher may have been the right thing for her to do under those conditions.

But in the presentations she's giving for work, she's mostly speaking to her colleagues or her direct reports, and the formality she's choosing isn't serving her.

So Annie may use industry jargon that her team uses on a daily basis, but she couldn't use that language if she were speaking to a broader audience. Her company might have specific slide templates and culture, but that wouldn't necessarily translate well to a different group of people.

As a speaker, you need to know which genre you are preparing for and adapt accordingly. Annie was uncomfortable in the genre she currently presents in, and it doesn't align with her presentation skills as they existed. But now she knows she has to close the gap, and it will take practice and time to get there.

Even if your style doesn't align with a specific genre, you can still be successful in it. As long as you understand the rules and norms of the genre, through study and iteration, you can make the jump. Remember, speaking is habitual, so this idea of learning a new genre is about building a new muscle. You can do it. And once you have, you can speak on any platform effectively.

## Genre Rules Can Be Broken

Arguably, every speaking genre comes with some rules or norms. A keynote talk should be aspirational. A TED talk is delivered without notes. A workshop should have specific learning objectives. But sometimes, you can break a rule, especially within genres. Speaking is a creative form, and we certainly don't want every talk or presentation to feel the same. How dreadfully dull.

But when you break a rule, you must first understand the rule and its purpose. Picasso spent years learning to paint like the old masters and could create paintings that were realistic and obeyed the rules of the art form. It was only after he mastered the rules that he broke them. Here's an example from our world, and while it may be small, we positively cringe when we see it happen.

Ever watched a panel discussion at a conference or some other event? Did you ever notice the chairs? There are the comfy low chairs that look like they came straight from Pottery Barn. Or there are the director's chairs straight from a movie set. Or (gasp) bar stools! Did you consider at all how the chairs affected the speakers?

Maybe the event organizers think these chairs look great on the stage. Or maybe they just think it fits the genre of "panel." But they never seem to notice how carefully the women have to sit on bar stools so that they maintain their modesty. Or how speakers are encouraged to slouch in a lounge chair designed for a living room.

Blythe went to see a beloved cookbook author speak. A man interviewed her, and they were both in these high back chairs—the only things other than a small table that were on a huge stage in a large auditorium. The interviewer seemed relaxed, leaning back into the chair, with his legs crossed. But the (short) author looked like she was in agony—she perched herself carefully at the edge of the chair so she could sit up and her feet could touch the floor, but she was constantly readjusting and just never seemed comfortable. It seemed like the chairs were meant to evoke a fireside chat, but instead of being cozy and welcoming, the unintended result was that the audience felt uncomfortable along with the author the whole time.

So, if you're on a panel, check out those chairs before you arrive or ask for a photo of the setup a few days in advance. Advocate for yourself if you can. Don't be afraid to break the rule that they've established. *You* have to sit on that awkward stool with no back, intended for tall men in pants, when you are a shorter female planning to wear a skirt.

As with any situation, you have to know the rules before you can break them. Once you do, though, imagine the other rules that you can slightly bend for the benefit of your performance or the audience's enjoyment. It's way better than putting the audience in a position to see a speaker sit awkwardly for an hour.

**Genres**

Individual Classroom Presentation

Group Classroom Presentation

Team Presentation

Keynote

TED or TEDx (or TED-like) Talk

Event Emcee / Host

Panel Moderator

Panelist

Fireside Chat

Legal Testimony

Legislative Testimony

Debate

Media Interview (TV, Podcast, Radio)

Board Report

Grand Rounds (Hospitals)

Venture Capital Pitch

Networking Elevator Pitch

Orals Defense of a Business Bid

School Assembly Announcement

Graduation Speech

Eulogy

Toast

Roast

Job Interview

Investor Call

Academic Defense (PhD)

Proposal Presentation

Medical License Renewal Interview

Pharmaceutical Trial Investigator Meeting

Introduction

Award Presentation

Ribbon Cutting

## Takeaway

As you can see from the extensive (and probably still incomplete) list of genres, there's a lot of nuance involved in this seemingly simple threshold concept. You need not be an expert in each of these situations. But by pausing to even *consider* how your style and the expectations of the genre do or don't align, you increase your chances of being more engaging and resonating in any speaking environment.

# Best Practices for Genre

Our mantra for genre:

**"Make no assumptions."**

While understanding genre is the most straightforward of the concepts, it is also often skipped, especially in its detail. As a speaker, asking as many questions as possible of your hosts, event planners, company leaders or peers hosting meetings may feel imposing. But the reverse is true. Your inquiries can help bring them clarity on their goals, and in turn help make your talk or speech that much more relevant and productive.

### Strategies to Advance Understanding of Genre

- Define the genre! Remember that content from a previous talk may or may not easily translate to a new genre.
- Ask about the purpose of the event and expectations.
- Determine the number of people and the level of the audience.
- Clarify the timing allowed, and if there is an expectation to include Q&A.

*(continued)*

(*continued*)

- Ask for a preparation call with panelists and the moderator, if appropriate.

- Ask for a rehearsal in the venue and stage setup (check those chairs, the height of the podium, and all the technology there to support you).

- Bend the rules when you believe the expectations don't match the genre. And run the idea by someone else if you do.

# 5

# Speaking Is Embodied

Speakers often think that speaking is all about what you say. But speaking isn't just about words. And it's not just about thoughts. The whole body is active when we speak. It incorporates the breath, posture, musculature, behavior, and expression. In many cases, this *embodiment* allows for the brain to make different connections.

Nothing explains it better than a speaker struggling to get to the embodied state:

**Speaker:**  "I practiced the talk last night and it still isn't feeling right."

**Coach:**  "Oh . . . so how does it feel?"

**Speaker:**   "Eh, it feels finished but I don't love it."
            (thoughtful pause)

**Coach:**     "Have you actually practiced it *out loud* yet?"

There are three responses we normally get to that question:

1. "Wait. WHAT?! I HONESTLY NEVER THOUGHT TO DO THAT."
2. "No, not yet, just been too busy."
3. "Sort of. I read it out loud but I didn't like it so I stopped working on it. I know, I know. But it is just so painful."

Just like you can't think your way into a great soccer goal or a football touchdown, you cannot just think your way into a great presentation.

When you say words out loud that you've outlined or written, it may feel awkward. Probably messy (remember that whole principle?). And you almost never like it the first time it comes out. And this is one problem *you cannot think your way out of.*

We don't really trust our clients to practice out loud (don't tell them that). So we'll ask some gentle questions (unlike the very direct one above) to discern if they are trying to fake a practice.

*"How did it sound?"*
*"How long did it take you?"*
*"Did you record it? Or listen back?"*

Speaking is not just words in your head or even those you may have written down; it is the act of *delivering those words with sound and accompanying non-verbal behaviors.*

This may seem obvious, but recognizing that *speaking is embodied* is a critical threshold to embrace to become a great communicator. We know that people take meaning from our words thanks to non-verbals that accompany them. What we sound like *and* what we look like when they are articulated, matter.

If you said happily or excitedly, "Last week someone stole my car," we would naturally think something was wrong with you (or your car) and likely question your credibility. Unless you're about to tell us a story that is full of adventure.

The same would be true if you somberly and quietly announced, "Last night I won a billion-dollar lottery."

These examples may seem silly, but we see it all the time. The speaker who reads a list of thank-yous with so little inflection it's hard to believe they feel gratitude. Or the leader who says how excited they are about a new initiative with a poker face that leaves you wondering, "Are they really?"

In any of these situations an audience will take pause to wonder, because what they just saw and what they heard convey totally opposite messages. While they might not think about any of this on a conscious level, they are probably taking it in. And if your delivery doesn't match your words, you can erode the trust between you and your audience.

What an audience wants is for your inside-out delivery to be consistent—what you are feeling, what you are saying, and how you say it are all aligned. This is what we mean by **congruence**, or the ability to connect your intention and message by understanding how your voice, your body language, your words, and your emotions integrate for your final delivery.

All of this embodiment is much harder than it seems for many, especially those in a deeply co-dependent relationship with the written word. Even in writing this book, we've become a lot more attuned to how much each word counts, but rarely have we spoken them out loud. Probably because the intention is for a reader to receive them, not a listener.

In summary, we love to remind speakers and communicators there is a moment when words you have been writing or thinking need to be *said*. Out loud. With your whole being. *To someone*. Not just yourself.

Ruth's next story is a perfect illustration of what can happen when someone, no matter how accomplished, fails to take this crucial step.

---

### Ruth: Having It Down

In 2010, I was invited to coach six speakers in the marketing department of a national healthcare products corporation. They loved the "new" TEDx style and wanted to host two hours of Ted-like talks from industry experts speaking at their annual retreat.

One was undeniably a leader in her field. She had written several books on her topic and was on a regular speaker circuit. But during her talk, it appeared as though she never really practiced or prepared. She stumbled from one idea to the next, forgot a section and looked rather lost.

Afterward, I asked her, "What happened? We reviewed your talk together during two different coaching sessions but it felt like it didn't stick!"

She replied, "I paced around my house for days reading and memorizing the talk. I thought I had it down."

*Ahhh.* "Having it down" meant in her mind, the words flowed as she read the page. She never practiced without the script in front of her.

So in short, it was a piece of written material that she was reading and failed to memorize. (News flash: Unless you are a trained actor, you will almost always fail to memorize a talk and deliver it like it's fresh.)

She never really embodied it. Ruth sees this person frequently and continually hears, even fifteen years later, how seminal that moment was for her in changing her speaking practice. Dare we say she never tried to "memorize" anything again.

The more we coach, the more we know this threshold concept to be true. We have witnessed too many "*Aha!*" moments when we nudge (or push) our clients to make this a part of their preparation. And, as you'll read, it's relatively easy to get started.

# You Must Decide to Stop Talking About the Talk and Deliver It

Often speakers will tell us about what they have decided to say but resist actually practicing delivering it with us. *Hmmm.* This means it's still just thoughts in their head, not an actual talk with a beginning, ending, story structure, data and more. And everything sounds better in your head.

A speaker must process their communication goals, the event's objective, the expected audience, the genre, their time limit, the boundaries of the venue, and technology (projection, sound, lights). So there must be a time when speakers move *from the thinking to the delivering*.

When we are coaching speakers, there is a moment where we will say:

*"Today we stop talking about it. Let's hear it."*

We usually get a blank stare of panic.

*"Oh I'm not really ready but . . . I guess I could try."*

Speakers then stumble into an opening, muddle through some stories, try to recall data and maybe stand up a call to action/closing. Hearing yourself literally *stumble* ignites a little (or a lot?) of anxiety.

After all, thoughts are rarely linear (if yours are, congratulations, you have a rare superpower!). Our brain makes lightning-fast connections between ideas and concepts. Speaking, on the other hand, must be linear to be understood.

Delivering the talk is about aligning your thoughts with your mouth. Every time you speak it, it improves your delivery. If you don't believe us, we nod to James McCroskey's study on the "rule of six" that when a speaker actually delivered a talk six times, it improved their memory retention, confidence, fluency and overall led to better audience engagement.[1]

There's a good reason for this. When you first learn a new task, your efforts are usually slow, stilted, and require a good deal of concentration.

Allow us to take you back to the first time you got behind a wheel to learn to drive. Each movement you made took time. You drove slowly because you were using all of your concentration to coordinate your hands, feet, eyes, to just make the car move. Especially if you learned on a stick shift! You probably struggled to find that sweet spot with the clutch, jerked the wheel, hit the brakes too hard, and scared the daylights out of your parents.

But as you kept driving, your movements became fluid and eventually you stopped thinking about it. Which leaves you free to keep your attention on the traffic around you.

This is muscle memory—the ability to reproduce a particular movement without conscious thought. And you can only get it by physically repeating the movement. Athletes use muscle memory to perform at their peak. Actors use muscle memory to remember their lines. And speakers can use muscle memory to allow them to spend more time connecting with the audience and less time thinking about what words they need to say.

So to all those speakers who say they aren't ready, we say: just try. We promise you that ripping off that band-aid isn't as painful as your brain wants you to think. Here, Blythe recounts a familiar story for us—one that any of us could have told, because we've all experienced this part of the process with nearly every client we've had. And the outcome is almost always the same.

## Blythe: The Chorus of Resistance

Since the pandemic, we've been coaching a large (think 75–100) cohort of speakers for an international conference. When we get to the part in the process when they have to actually *talk the talk*, embody the words, lift the words from the outline into being; people are normally prepared for this. We've reminded them at the end of the second call that this is the next step. We've sent them a reminder email letting them know the expectation of the third call.

On one particular call, four people show up, and there is a chorus:

*"I'm not as far as I want to be."*

*"It's not good."*

*"Uhhhh . . . I don't really have the talk ready."*

And one person is quiet.

I push them anyway. I remind them that this is a safe space and it's okay to fail. But then something crazy starts to happen. The first person who goes has said something like, "I'm not ready at all," except words fall into place as they speak just from their outline and notes. A little magic in the making.

The next individual goes and was the one who hadn't said anything self-deprecating at the top of the call, and it's rocky, but they get through.

It's not a huge surprise then, that the next speaker takes her turn, and it's dreadful and there are false starts, redos, long pauses, and heavy sighs. She is deeply frustrated.

And then it's over and they're through the worst, and they each have accomplished something very real—they have embodied their talk, some of them for the first time. And as a result, they make important realizations. (This is the best part!)

*"I don't need this information; it's detracting from the idea."*

*"I'm getting stuck on the transitions."*

*"I think this section works better somewhere else."*

*"That went better than I expected."*

Some finally understand the importance of the opening hook, others forgot to include a call to action, others just need a conclusion to a simple example or story. All great takeaways from saying the words out loud. Things they might not have realized if not for this exercise.

Skipping this step of embodiment just means you are stepping into a performance unrehearsed, which is like heading into a competition with no training. This step is what makes speaking, *speaking*. And there is no substitute.

## Narrative Transitions Usually Only Happen When the Talk Is Delivered

Because speech is fleeting, audiences need speakers to be a "narrative guide" not dissimilar from a tour guide in an art museum. They give you a preview of what's next, you will move to that piece of art, they will explain that art's significance and then sum it up and preview the next one.

This means the speaker must segment and organize specific cues like the old-fashioned "I'm going to tell you this today . . . " or "Let me recap what I said."

These small bridges that allow an audience to know you are shifting between points are critical for the listener—yet often ignored.

Here a few:

*First,*
*Next up,*
*On the other hand,*
*It reminds me of,*
*Moving on,*
*So . . .*

Not surprisingly, our speakers ask for help with transitions on every call.

But they don't usually happen until the end of the work on a talk.

Transitions tie a talk together like a ribbon on a present.

Once all of the content is organized, delivery is in progress and a speaker begins to understand what the audience needs to be "guided." It isn't as easy as writing where a hard period, paragraph, or chapter break allows a reader to think about the transitions in the story in their
own
sweet
time.

## Performances Aren't Just for Theater

How enjoyable would a speaker be whom you can't hear, can't see, or can't understand? Speaking of any type requires physical presence, good breath support and engagement with the audience, leading us to the notion that speaking is indeed *performative*.

Stick with us here. We know performance can be a controversial topic. In today's culture, authenticity is valued, and at first glance, performance might seem to be the opposite. But ask any actor and they will tell you that a good performance is authentic. They spend years honing their craft so that their performances are true and natural.

So, if you as a speaker acknowledge the performative aspect of speaking, there is a lot you can learn from the way actors train to do it. There are two general categories of how actors bring a character to life.

The first is to work *inside out*. Investigate how a character feels. Think about their backstory. Connect personal experiences to the given circumstances of the character.

In this way, the actor transforms themself into the character.

The second general style is to work from the *outside in*. To focus on movement and gesture and vocal choices.

Both styles can create authentic performances.

Even though speakers are not creating a character, these two approaches can still be helpful as they near the moment they stand in front of their audience to speak. Their performative moment.

Some speakers benefit from working insde-out first, digging in to discover what they really want to accomplish, how they feel about what they are sharing, and how they hope the audience will respond. This kind of work can allow them to perform their talks with deep authenticity.

But for some speakers, this approach doesn't work. No matter how much they understand how they feel about their content, they just can't seem to convey that passion with the world. For these people, there is always the outside-in approach. By focusing on technical changes to their voice or body, their performance comes to life.

It's important to add that there is no such thing as perfection in performance. In fact, when Noam Chomsky first introduced the idea of linguistic performance, he included in that idea " . . . specific utterances made by the native speaker of a language, including false starts, hesitations and speech errors."[2]

We love that part about errors—authentic speaking performance includes plenty of them. Ruth hangs her hat as the non-perfectionist in the group and she's super-proud of it. Indeed, our entire practice rests on "Done is better than perfect." Moreover, she reflects: "It wasn't until I was a sophomore in college that I got my first A—in anything—and it happened to be in Public Speaking." (The rest is history and this book you are now reading.)

When people call us and ask us to help them be a better speaker, we always reply: When you have an audience, a date and place where you will speak, then call us. Why? Because you never have adrenaline without a deadline. And a key component of performance is that pressure, managing the excitement and anxiety in the moment that you will need to deliver a talk.

And performance adrenaline has its benefits. It allows you to think on your feet, making adjustments when things go sideways. When harnessed, it can also give you the presence and energy it takes to command the stage. If you "prepare a talk for no particular reason for no particular person," then you'll usually find a reason to reschedule a dozen times since there's no consequence waiting for you on a certain day.

While we were supporting another big business pitch with a team of eight people, the leader told the group the day before the pitch, "Don't worry. This isn't a performance." We could tell she was trying to reduce the anxiety the word "performance" brings. But everyone knew it *was* a performance and one that was being scored with a panel of judges like gymnastics at the Olympics. And so we prepared the team rigorously, as we do all our clients.

After the pitch, they agreed that had they NOT rehearsed and NOT prepared like it was a performance, they wouldn't have done so well in what really ended up feeling like a planned conversation. That's what makes a speaker "look like a natural"—*when they are truly prepared and grounded for the moment.*

For them, and for you, the pressure to perform leads to better habits and, ultimately, impact and delivery. Considering other aspects of performance can also enhance communication. Acacia shares a particularly memorable choice she witnessed.

---

### Acacia: Taking the Audience on a Journey

Early in my career as a trainer, I had a pivotal moment while observing a mentor's facilitation style. I was just a newbie in my training and development career, leading my first workshops and training sessions. I was building new habits every day, trying to soak up everything I could.

One day, as I'm watching my mentor, I noticed something strange: as she began weaving a story, she purposefully moved to the back of the room. It seemed counterintuitive to me. Eye contact is critical in public speaking, and she lost it as the participants couldn't look at her without craning their necks.

Curiosity piqued, I pondered her choice. I realized that her goal in that moment was to immerse participants in the narrative, encouraging them to visualize themselves within the scenario rather than watch her. So she, rather dramatically, removed herself from their view.

And it worked! Attendees became thoughtful as she spoke. Some closed their eyes to really picture themselves in her story. I got goosebumps as the energy in the room shifted. She knew exactly what she was doing. She adjusted her performance for that specific moment. This moment taught me to never forget the importance of performance when speaking.

Just like any good actor, Acacia's mentor knew that every move we make when we speak is a choice—whether we make the decision consciously or not. That's what makes it a performance. And we need to understand why we are making those choices to be a compelling communicator.

## Dress Rehearsals Are the Final Inning of Embodiment

It is proven—at least through the thousands of speakers we have coached—that doing a dress rehearsal in the very theater, conference room, or other venue where you are going to deliver a presentation will eliminate 50% of the nerves you may be experiencing. Of course, there is no scientific study to prove this (if there is, apologies to the researcher who owns this data), except to say in our experience, speakers who do *not* utilize a day-before in-venue rehearsal are usually less prepared for the actual presentation.

Why is this? Let us count the ways . . .

**Visualization of your audience:** In the event venue, you can see where they will sit, how many may be there, and how to engage them with your stage movements. Even showing up to a board room for a smaller presentation to see how to look at the executives while also managing your slides is an important step to practice.

**Knowing where the camera is:** A lot of presentations are recorded. Knowing how to engage with the camera will give you a much better video for YouTube or your speaker reel. We used to tell TEDx speakers that only a small portion of your audience will be in front of you in the theater. The rest will be online watching your talk later. A quick on-camera tip: Frequent pacing and large movements on a video can be distracting; the TED conference's own advice is to stay as still as possible.

**Being done:** Nothing says "put your pencil down" better than a well-executed dress rehearsal. Many idea generators, entrepreneurs, and writers *love* to iterate and keep revising. But at some point, that work must cease! Better it be a dress rehearsal than the day of when you arrive rushed, stressed, and still writing. You and your audience will know you didn't do your best work at that moment.

**Being within time:** A stage manager, event planner, or key executive in charge of the meeting will want to know one major thing the day before: *Are you staying within your allotted time?* Sometimes speakers don't know until they present the whole talk. Remember: "In the boxing match of time vs. content, time always wins."

**Affirming you "got this":** Going through a full dress rehearsal is the best nod of confidence you can give yourself. Afterwards, you can focus on exercise, sleep, and enjoying the experience.

One final note: if you don't have access to the venue to practice, block time with a colleague or friend the day before to practice *wherever you are*. We don't want your first "practice" to be on stage, in front of your audience, the day of your event. That's not practicing. That's delivering, and they are two very different things.

If anything unexpected comes up during the dress rehearsal, take a moment to work on it, fix whatever is necessary, and build it into your muscle memory, just like Acacia's client, Jane, does in our next story.

---

### Acacia: 30 Seconds to Own the Stage

I was working with a client (I'll call her Jane) for a major keynote.

Jane is a national expert in her field. And she was ready and eager to make a living giving keynotes. I was helping her prepare for her first big paid one.

She'd put so much pressure on herself, she actually struggled to walk on stage with confidence.

She was over-rehearsed, nervous, worried she would fail, and she carried all of that with her. Sky-high

*(continued)*

(*continued*)

expectations combined with extreme effort and catastrophizing can debilitate any speaker. She had a lot of what we call "head trash," unhelpful thoughts that get in the way.

So I decided to get her out of her head and into her body. At our rehearsal, we focused on the crucial first 30 seconds of her talk. How she could visualize it before she walked on. How she would walk on the stage and take a breath before she started. How she could take her nervous energy and use it to push her feet into the ground for a strong, commanding presence. How she could really look at the audience, make eye contact, and connect.

She was almost like a car that didn't want to start— but once she did, I knew she'd be off to the races.

With each rehearsal, she witnessed her transformation—from tentative steps to a confident stride, from hesitant gestures to a commanding presence.

We fine-tuned her delivery, pausing after each repetition to reflect and refine what worked and what didn't (see Principle #6). And with each new attempt, she became more assured, more engaging, *more herself*.

For Acacia's client, this wasn't about putting on a façade or becoming some perfect version of herself; it was about discovering how to embody her message authentically.

She loved her job; she just needed to access that passion. True authenticity on stage stems from dedicated practice, allowing you to express your genuine self with clarity and conviction.

**Takeaway**

The next time you step onto that stage, whether it's a literal stage or simply a presentation in front of your team, remember: it's not about aiming for a perfection that doesn't really exist; it's about unleashing the best version of yourself. The best way to do that is to bring your whole self. And that includes your voice and your physicality. By bringing embodiment into your preparation, you can truly do that.

Only after you've done all that preparation can you heed the last words of advice we give speakers before they take the stage: "Have fun!"

# Best Practices for Embodiment

Our embodiment mantra:

**"Practice. Out loud."**

It is still mystifying to us that people think they can write a speech or talk and not practice it out loud. Trust us on this. Nothing else works.

## Be Yourself

Your audience doesn't want you to be anyone else. It may take practice to bring out your *best* self, but always be yourself.

Here's the hidden secret: don't apologize. If you aren't a great speaker, you may explain it isn't your favorite thing to do but never say you are sorry. Do the best you can and let the audience savor the gifts you do bring. Don't distract them otherwise.

In the thousands of talks we've heard, we prefer someone who is an average speaker with a great idea over a superior speaker with a horrible one. We're uninterested in cookie-cutter speakers. We want to hear great ideas shared in diverse styles. Speaking is hard and mastering it is harder. But that doesn't mean you still can't represent who you are in the moment. Audiences will discern when you are over-indexing the wrong way to try to be too performative, too funny, too perfect.

When a talent manager or business leader hires us to help one of their executives, inevitably there is ONE thing that is holding them back in their communication style. However, they always tell us, "We don't need you to turn this person into something they aren't." Rest assured, as much as we might try, there's little chance we could.

**Strategies toward embodiment:**

- Practice. Out loud. A lot. (Can we say this any more?)
- Try it on your feet too, if you're giving it in person.
- Build muscle memory by practicing with your clicker if there are slides.
- Record your practice. Listen back. Video it. Watch it back.
- When transitioning to a new section within a talk, focus on a key word or phrase to help you make the bridge. Highlight those within your outline and give those moments extra attention when you practice.
- Instead of editing a written script (see Principle #2), spend your time *speaking it out*.
- Don't pass up an opportunity for a dress rehearsal. All manner of questions will be clarified by being in the venue and practicing your talk one more time.
- Become familiar with your stress responses which may get in the way of your full embodiment. A full set of strategies can be found in the Advanced Skills section.

# 6

# Successful Speaking Requires Feedback

One of our dear friends, Larry Smith, the author of the *Six Word Memoir* series, was a speaker at one of our TEDx events. When we showed him these threshold concepts in a draft, he reacted to this one on feedback pretty viscerally.

"Everyone tells you you need to get feedback, especially to record yourself and listen back. But when you actually made me do it, it was one of the *hardest but most productive things* I've ever done in preparing a talk. Period."[1] He reflected that the experience permanently changed the way he prepares.

Let's dig into it. Why is feedback so important?

Because of the *social and temporal (fleeting) nature* of speaking, and since we cannot actually listen to ourselves speak in real time, *external feedback* is essential for continued improvement. Not only improvement of a specific message, but also improvement as a speaker overall.

We can accept you don't want to do *any* of this feedback work. That's okay. You are not alone.

*"Excuse me, let me stop reading and open my Voice Memo (recording) app on my phone to record myself . . . and listen back right now."*

*Said no one ever.*

We're familiar with this feeling. Blythe worked with a client (not the only one we've ever had!) who didn't think he needed feedback, and probably didn't really want it, either.

---

### Blythe: From Reluctant to Eager

When speakers are sent to us from their organizations to prepare for a meeting or event, they're normally tickled to get speaking coaching. Coaching on someone else's budget? Sounds great! Occasionally, on the other hand, we'll get a speaker who is very busy, speaks all the time, and doesn't think the time is worth it. And yes, to some people a four-hour commitment over the course of a month can be a significant investment. But if, at the end of that time, you have crafted a compelling and successful talk and you've learned something new in the process, it can be a worthwhile investment.

Anyway, Dave was a "very busy person." I had heard rumblings that he was unwilling to schedule his sessions, and that if he didn't want to continue the coaching after the first call, he didn't have to.

I was nervous going into the call. I didn't know what to expect. When we first hopped on Zoom, I asked him to tell me a little bit about himself, and instead, he turned it around and said, "Why don't you tell me what this process is all about?"

Briefly I explained the process: each of the calls are an hour or less and they build on each other. There's at least a week between calls to write, iterate, and practice. I assured him that this is his talk and I was here to help keep him on track, not to tell him what to say.

Still seeming a little skeptical, he then jumped in and said, "Well, this sounds like it could be really useful to me—maybe I could learn something about the other talks I give, not just this one." And right then and there, he committed to the whole process without a hitch.

He surprisingly leaned in, and he didn't just take the four hours we agreed to, he also reached out to me between calls asking for my input and feedback. All it took was a willingness.

People who don't get feedback regularly might not know how useful it can be. And not just for one talk—sometimes what you learn is usually applicable well into the future for other talks.

All that said, it's not lost on us that we are one of many (thousands?) who have written on the subject of feedback. We did, however, find the article that summarized the research studies on feedback given in educational settings—like when learning to speak—and will sum it up in this sentence:

"This evidence [of all the studies] shows that although [general learning] feedback is among the major influences, the *type* of feedback and the *way* it is given can be *differentially effective*. [emphasis added]"[2] In other words, don't just ask for general feedback from no one in particular.

Here's what you need to encounter about feedback in learning to speak:

First, you must be open to feedback, both yours and others. Feedback must be aligned with your goals, and the context of the intended audience. And indeed, as the research study cited above declared, the style and timing of feedback matters. Your audience *will* evaluate you at some level, so it's best to get into that feedback habit early.

## Useful Feedback Aligns the Goal of the Speaker with the Perspective of the Audience

You might be thinking (here's hoping), "I'm on board for feedback. Bring it on!" Most of our clients are usually eager for feedback on their presentations. They go through their decks, share their data, give a call to action, and then turn to us and say, "What did you think?"

We know better than to take the bait and answer such a broad question.

As a speaker about to get feedback, it is your job to detail the goals of your communication and the intended audience. If you don't, you may get feedback that is not helpful. Let's look at the kinds of feedback you may get. You might hear back about . . .

- message (data/facts)
- stories (emotion)
- tone
- speed
- breathing
- body language
- slides/visuals
- energy

Those giving you feedback may just have opinions based on how they are feeling, but if they don't know what you want to achieve, the feedback can be less than helpful.

Now, once in a while we find ourselves in a little bit of a double bind. When we are hired by companies to coach speakers for town halls and other consequential meetings, our job is to coach the speaker to the needs of the event and their goal. But sometimes, there may be internal staff listening in to the calls. This can be very productive, helping to level set the goals of the event, timing and technology. It can also pose conflicts if the staff person has a certain agenda, one that is unknown to the speaker, and gives feedback in that spirit. The speaker is left in a difficult position as they try to navigate conflicting feedback. Blythe shares one such story here.

## Blythe: Managing Feedback

Once a year, an awesome organization reaches out to us to coach speakers for a big event. I've done it three years in a row now, and I have met and learned from the most remarkable individuals, who are doing truly incredible work in the world and are experienced speakers. Over the course of six weeks, I weave in and out of their hectic schedules and work with them on their talks for this event.

We tie the talks to the theme of the event, and tell what can sometimes be very complex stories and ideas simply. Finally, we arrive at the content review, a rehearsal of sorts, which typically happens about five days to a week before the event. It's a last pass for the speaker to build confidence and a time for specific, structured feedback. Our intention is never to blow up a talk so close to the event, but to give positive encouragement and make small tweaks where necessary.

After all, between the content review and the event, the speaker should just be practicing saying the talk out loud and building confidence.

We invite event organizers to the content review so they can build scripts around the talks for introductions and transitions, and so there are no surprises. I ask everyone in attendance to respond to a few prompts, which should have the effect of streamlining the kind of feedback the speaker is getting. We're looking for narrow feedback: Is the talk landing, are the transitions connecting the ideas, and has the speaker said anything that will cause the audience to stop listening?

But there's one person who takes this opportunity, mere days away from the event, to nit-pick on content and the structure of talks. They bring into question all of the decisions the speaker has made up to this point. Every time. And it has a predictable effect: the speaker becomes self-conscious, worries, starts to question their entire talk, and then I become defensive on their behalf.

Don't get me wrong. Feedback is essential to improving your speaking, so I'm not pooh-poohing feedback. But let's take a moment to think about what this feedback giver was trying to accomplish. It turned out to be entirely about what message THEY want to share with the audience. It's like they're saying, "Don't talk about apples, talk about zebras."

If you want to avoid being this person, keep your feedback focused on reflecting back to the speaker what you actually heard. Let *them* decide if that was the message they wanted to share. And as a speaker asking for feedback who doesn't have a coach like one of us to advocate on your behalf, be specific about what you're looking for at any point in the process, so the feedback you receive can be helpful and beneficial to your process instead of sending you off the rails.

It's not just the goal of the talk that matters when giving and receiving feedback. The feedback needs to align with the perspective of the intended audience. A speaker cannot really get into the audience's mind. And their perspective matters most. (Remember, it's not what you say; it's what people hear that matters.)

This means that if you're soliciting feedback, share with a trusted listener whom you're talking to and what you think they are expecting. And when *you're* giving feedback, think about what the intended audience would want to hear. What questions are on their mind? What do they think and feel about the topic?

For instance, when we work with large groups of data and analytics speakers, we know that the audience is interested in hearing about code and deep specificity in how they solved a programming issue. Those topics are not always relatable to us as coaches. But we're seasoned pros at coaching in subject areas that are not our own. In those moments, it is our job to make a concerted effort to get into the mind of the audience. We look for clarity, delivery, timing, and accessibility (not too much jargon) to help the speaker affirm that their audience can follow along.

Ruth had the pleasure of helping another technical speaker connect with multiple audiences as she shares here:

## Ruth: Inclusive Design

One of my favorite coaching feedback stories came from working closely with an oncology clinician-scientist from a large hospital system. He gave an incredibly compelling TEDxColumbus talk outlining the steps he believed were needed to cure cancer. They addressed complex cellular and molecular behaviors which he'd been studying for decades.

There were people in the room who were scientists and researchers; they really wanted to see details and scientific evidence. There were many others who were not. And many had not been in a science class since high school. They wanted to understand the concept without too many alienating details. The question quickly became: How can he speak to the experts without alienating the lay folks?

This became a central consideration when giving him feedback. As such, he made some smart and creative decisions. First, he decided to label the technical names of the T-cells on the slides. Then, he agreed not to say many of those terms out loud. This allowed the scientific audience to see them in the visuals while not losing the lay audience in the spoken narrative. Had he used all of those very technical T-cell terms and acronyms, assuredly the audience would have lost the thread of his message.

For what it's worth, we never suggest that a speaker dumb down their content. It is truly about making it accessible to their audiences. That mindset shift will allow a very smart speaker with a lifetime of content the license to let go of needing to be the smartest person in the room. Rarely does that turn out well.

Understanding the perspective of an audience is not easy. And many who are happy to give feedback to speakers are not great at thinking about how a different person might hear a message. Even though it is hard to come by, understanding what your intended audience will take away from your talk is the most important feedback you can get.

## You Are Your Best Source of Feedback (Really)

So . . . who should give you feedback?

Surprisingly, *you as the speaker* need to be the first and most central provider of feedback to yourself.

*Why would the best feedback be what I give myself immediately after I have spoken?*

Here's why:

Whenever a speaker makes an attempt at delivering a talk, the first question we always ask is "How do you feel about it?" And almost all of the time, they have an immediate set of answers that addresses most of the issues we, as viewers/listeners, may have seen in the talk. Such as: "I rushed through it." Or, "I need an ending." Or, "I don't have my transitions finished." Or, "I don't like how that story came out in the middle." At the end of their reflection, we may tuck in one or two things they need to tweak, but as for the big stuff, they know what they need to work on.

As the late Bill Hart-Davidson, a beloved Rhetoric and Composition scholar, said in giving feedback to writers: " . . . when the teacher is the main source of feedback, well the teacher is learning a lot. But the students are not learning as much. Because *it's the givers* who gain most from the practice of framing high-quality feedback. [emphasis added]"[3]

Moreover, when we as speech coaches give the first and main feedback, the speakers are listening to how we feel, not always what they need to work on. It was the same when Ruth's kids were in pre-school and the teachers taught her and her husband never to tell their kids "good job." They heard "It's great," and thought "I'm done, let's go out and play now." They have learned something but not as much as they could if they *themselves* reflected on the assignment. The same holds true for speakers. If you want to be in true service to them, help them self-reflect. They learn something faster and more meaningful about the work ahead of them every single time.

So, how do you give feedback to yourself? If a speech coach isn't available to pull it out of you (or even when they are), audio and visual recordings are really the best way.

We know from certain forms of psychology that if you identify the issue you want to solve, you are far more likely to want to correct it than if someone tells you it is an issue to solve. When you record yourself, you are not only being witness to yourself, you are putting yourself in the shoes of your audience. Recording yourself forces you to move from *thinking about what you are going to say* to *saying it.* You will catch phrases, pacing, and timing that you otherwise would not, even if you speak into a mirror.

Case in point: this is one of Ruth's favorite stories to tell about a client who really needed to see to believe.

---

### Ruth: The Animated Corpse

In my years of coaching, this self-reflection may win the prize.

A senior official was recorded for a semi-live event, which means we helped coach him with a 10-minute talk that was recorded; it was then played back to a virtual audience followed by live questions with his CEO.

When he (finally) watched the video during the event, he told his staff:

*"I look like an animated corpse."*

Truth was, while he was being hard on himself, he wasn't entirely wrong. He was pale, stiff, and monotone. His content was compelling, but with a livelier delivery, it could have been captivating. There was indeed room for improvement.

We recommend that the first time you watch yourself on a recording is not mid-career, leaving you wondering "Have I always looked that way?"

---

The next coaching process with him was hard work. It involved many more painful moments of watching himself on video. We asked him to "overact" and talk in ways that made him feel, well, silly. But, because there was video evidence, he also got to see how he didn't really look silly. He could give himself the feedback that he was not doing too much.

And with practice, he learned to be engaging. Fortunately, far more than an animated corpse.

By the way, if you're trying to discover for yourself if you're "an animated corpse," we wholeheartedly do NOT recommend speaking to a mirror for practice. Just like watching your own square on Zoom, it's a recipe for self-consciousness. Watching yourself as you speak *is not natural*. It's impossible to give yourself feedback while you're in the middle of speaking. Instead, use a mirror to check your teeth and hair *before* you speak.

AI apps as a feedback tool fall somewhere between assessing your own recordings and depending on someone else for feedback. But because there is ultimately no human giving you the insights, the feedback you get from an AI tool is closest to self-feedback, since you will need to integrate the feedback on your own. They can help, providing recordings and minimal feedback as long as you use them with the understanding of their limitations. We've outlined what they do well and where they fall short in "Technology and Speaking" at the end of the book.

We're not saying that you are the only person you should solicit for feedback. After all, speaking is social (see Principle #3). But we do believe you should seek your own feedback first.

In short, *after* you have recorded yourself, listened and revised, seek someone to give you feedback that has the right context about your intended audience, timeframe, goal, and genre before they offer you any advice. Even better, since you've already given yourself feedback, it's a lot easier to ask for specific insights from others.

## The Timing and Format of Feedback Matters

Warning: this may feel dramatic. Feedback that is given at the wrong moment can affect a speaker's confidence for years to come.

Truth. We've seen it so many times.

A speaker comes to us and says, "Four years ago I got feedback on a presentation that has kept me from ever speaking again." Or, "No one ever told me how bad I was and it wasn't until my review months later when it was mentioned. I was so embarrassed. I wish I had known to make immediate changes."

Inadvertently asking for feedback at the wrong time or inviting folks to give feedback who don't have the whole context has some delicate consequences. Acacia's next story is a good example.

## Acacia: A Last-Minute Scramble

A friend of mine was one week out from delivering a keynote inside her own business when the event planners, some peers in an adjacent department, reached out saying, "Can we have a chat?" They had some notes.

Uh-oh.

During the call they shared how *they* wanted the speaker to deliver the content complete with a list of different messages, and very specific slides and exercises they wanted incorporated into the presentation.

While this feedback was not bad in and of itself, it had terrible timing.

I told her that she had the choice as a speaker to accept or decline their suggestions.

Now, my friend handled the situation like a courageous and patient pro, implementing the requested changes. This meant she didn't complain, she took a deep breath, found some time on her calendar (the biggest hurdle!) and pivoted the content of the talk. She knew that the best thing for her career, in that culture, was that this time she had to push through the discomfort and deliver a talk that really wasn't hers. It happens.

It took some time to jump over the hurdle of the request, remove content she had worked hard on, find natural places to tuck in the new content, and then become familiar with what was an entirely new talk.

*(continued)*

(*continued*)

And the talk went well. She hated the process and hopes it doesn't happen again (we gave her some tips to thwart future late-breaking changes). It begged a lesson about the importance of timing when providing feedback to speakers.

If you're ever lucky enough to be involved in a speaker's creative process, it's crucial to be considerate of *what* feedback you offer *when*. Big ideas and concepts need to be a part of the invitation or first rounds of drafts, not final stages when the talk is done.

Throughout the years we've become a lot more proactive about who is allowed to give feedback in a team's coaching preparation process—and when.

Here's why: we move teams on a journey, say for a big pitch, from chaos to clarity over a very rapid two weeks of sometimes daily coaching. If a third-party reviewer jumps in the middle of that week expecting the speakers to be further along than they are, it can be challenging, as the "side chatter" can cast doubt that the team is ready. This has happened to several of our cohorts before, and assuredly they were still working through many kinks.

We make sure that reviewers are aligned with the knowledge like this: "We know we need to get to the 9th inning by the end of the week, but this may feel like we're only in the 4th or 5th inning today. That's okay because we have time blocked to work through those final steps after this meeting."

Make sure if you are invited to give feedback to a team, that you understand their timeline and work done to get to that point. Please keep your bias in check about how much you think they should have completed. You never know how much more time and energy they have left to get to the finish line.

Lastly, it doesn't help anyone to backchannel feedback. Meaning, if you have something to say to a speaker, find a quiet time to ask about their process and what's left in the preparation. You can better balance out any anxiety you may be feeling versus the support the speakers need to be successful.

## Environments Must Be Safe for Feedback

Environments must be safe for feedback.

Okay let's break down that sentence, backwards.

Feedback = The process of giving reflections, positive or negative, but hopefully with the intention of growth and improvement.

Safe = Where the speaker, who is receiving the feedback, feels as if she or he is *being cared for*.

Environment = This is organizational culture + timing + location.

In other words, is it accepted practice by a company or organization to give constructive feedback? Is there a consideration to when it is given and where?

Amy Edmonson, a Harvard professor, researcher, and scholar on issues of leadership and organizational learning, explains at the core of this problem is a hidden but powerful element: psychological safety. She pioneered the understanding of the role psychological safety plays in the workplace and defines it as the degree to which the work environment is safe for interpersonal risk taking.[4]

This is incredibly important when you're talking about feedback that is related to a person's speaking style and presence, as speaker feedback often is. Acacia shares a story about what can happen when this psychological safety is absent.

Since speaking is risky already, that environment *around feedback* is essential. A culture where it's genuinely invited, given, and accepted. One that also acknowledges that speaking is social and messy and says, "We don't expect you to get this perfect or right the first time."

---

### Acacia: First, Do No Harm

Poorly delivered feedback, without psychological safety, can do damage.

I was working with a rising executive at a Fortune 500 company who had recently taken on a new role. It demanded she be able to deliver presentations to a huge variety of audiences in a way that was engaging and authentic. During our style and delivery workshop, I noticed immediately that this would be a challenge.

Her presentation style was stilted, monotone, and lacking in personality. When I looked at her eyes as she spoke, they actually seemed dead. We recorded her so she could listen and watch. She could see it too. And yet, she really struggled to implement any changes we tried.

A week later, she revealed to me that her whole family was surprised to learn that she was monotone at work. At home, she is quick to smile and laugh. When I asked what was different for her at work, she said "I need to be serious and professional at work."

"Sometimes," I said. "But also, who tells you that?"

I expected her to talk about her own self-imposed expectations. Instead, her eyes filled with tears.

She told me about a manager she had early in her career. This manager repeatedly told her that her light-hearted demeanor was unacceptable. That she needed to be more "professional" and act more "seriously."

What the leader probably didn't know, is that this feedback spoke directly to all the fears this young professional had. Having come from a rough background and making her way in the workplace without the usual master's degrees, she always felt like she didn't belong. And this leader was telling her exactly that. That who she was wasn't okay.

So she learned to hide who she was at work.

No wonder she was monotone and lacked expression.

The initial feedback she was given might have been given for good reason, and might have even been given with the best of intentions. But it was uninvited. And it was extremely personal—she was the only person on the team given regular feedback on her style.

A stark lesson emerged in how to give feedback on someone's style. Take your time to build trust. Be gentle. Let them observe themselves. Or bring in a professional. Because, while sometimes feedback is uncomfortable, it should never do harm.

How to do this? First, make it routine. When feedback is an expected part of the process there is a time and place to give and receive it. It becomes normalized.

Second, make it inviting. This means don't ask, "Can I give you some feedback?" Rather, ask humble inquiry questions about what they are working on, where they may be stuck, what the genre is, and let them know you are willing to help. Ideally, they'll ask for the feedback in the end.

If you don't know the person, all bets are off. There are no established rules or culture around offering up your opinions to strangers. Keep the feedback to yourself. Ruth learned this lesson the hard way.

---

### Ruth: A Hard Lesson

Within two months, I saw a paid keynote speaker speak live at two different conferences. She was someone who was very sought after on the speaking circuit, complete with a best-selling book. But she was, in my listening-in-real-time experience, hard to follow because—pause—she never took a breath. We like speakers who are easy to listen to. Even if the words are delivered quickly, our brains require a moment to process the knowledge. This speaker never gave her audience a moment to think.

I am not an active tweeter (when it was Twitter), but I tagged her in a post that said:

> "@hername LOVED your content, again. Second time in 2 months to see you live. Keep up the great work but don't be afraid to take a breath."

---

I immediately got a DM back, and I'm paraphrasing:

*"Whoever the hell you are, you have no business or license to slam me like that in public. Piss off."*

I felt properly chastened. And I still feel (a little) bad about it to this day. But she had a point. For all of my beliefs about feedback, I should have known better than to offer unsolicited feedback.

Even though she gets paid $30–40K for her 45-minute keynote. Even though she was on a stage before an audience of hundreds. Even though she could step into greatness if she paused. And even though we could argue that she might have accepted it with a growth mindset. None of this matters because I didn't have a relationship with her.

Needless to say, that was the first and last time I gave a speaker feedback on social media.

## Takeaway

You can tell we care a lot about feedback and the people who receive it. After all, it is a huge part of our job. And we know that receiving feedback is not only required to excel as a speaker, it is also a gift. As Amy Edmonson aptly reflects: "Finding out that you are wrong is even more valuable than being right, because you are learning."[5]

## Best Practices for Feedback

Our mantra for feedback:

**"Stay curious."**

Staying curious requires humility. You have to accept that there might be better ways to share your message. But when you remove yourself as the central character of the story and think of the feedback as a way of connecting the audience with the messages you want them to hear, the process gets easier.

Moreover, when you make it about yourself, your anxiety will increase as it will compound on itself.

But . . . feedback is inherently about you, your content and your performance. As you seek it, receive it, and give it, use these best practices for the most productive improvements.

### Strategies for Receiving Feedback

- Ask for specific feedback. Not "What did you think?" More "What did you think about X?"

- Let your feedback giver know what your goal is and to whom you will be speaking.

- Let your feedback giver know what you DO and DO NOT need/want feedback on.

- Say "thank you" to any feedback, even the bad stuff.

- Ask clarifying questions. "Can you tell me more about . . . ?"

- Remember to stay curious.

### Strategies for Giving Feedback

- Find out what the speaker wants feedback on.

- Tune your ears to the perspective of the intended audience, which may or may not be you.

- Try starting with questions to stay aligned with the speaker. We love to always ask first "How do you feel?" to give them a chance to release any tension.

- Do your best to keep feedback concise and refrain from telling stories about yourself.

- Listen carefully to their response to you: Did they hear you? Are they frustrated? Are they dismissive? Meet them where they are with compassion and safety that you are on their side.

- Indicate when you are sharing something that is just your opinion.

# Threshold Concepts Summary and Integrations

We can imagine you are asking WHERE and WHEN do I find time to integrate these threshold concepts?

Anytime you are engaging in the act of speaking, you are probably encountering these concepts. They are particularly useful to bring to the forefront of your mind whenever *learning* is happening.

We define *learning* broadly: it can be your own personal, individual development; learning that is organized at your workplace or a leadership program; or learning that takes place in both colleges and high schools.

Learning to be a great communicator is best when it's integrated with other subjects and ideas that you are passionate about. This is true of writing as well. As Elizabeth Wardle and other writing scholars have demonstrated, people learn to write in particular contexts where they use writing to accomplish particular goals. She has helped faculty from all disciplines see how they can take responsibility for teaching writing in their fields (see her article, "What Critics of Student Writing Get Wrong"[1]). She teaches professors of every field—from physics to history to supply chain management—how to help students learn to write using the genres and conventions they expect and use in their own work. If you looked up the writing requirement for a math major at Miami University, you would find a math proof class.

Likewise, we have no doubt that helping people to encounter threshold concepts for being a great speaker can happen inside existing classes, workshops, or events such as board meetings, town halls, conferences, or cumulative assessments like a PhD dissertation. Being a great communicator does not have a finish line; it is a continuous, lifelong process. Knowing each genre, audience, and situation will require different things. How can you integrate what you have learned in this book throughout your daily life—both personally and professionally—as a communicator?

Here are a few scenarios to spark ways to integrate practice into your daily life.

## Scenario #1

You just want to improve, period. Meaning, there isn't a moment coming up in your life when you have to present, but you know in general you want to get better. (We applaud you!)

Early in Ruth's coaching practice, she had a few people ask her to help them get better at speaking. But they didn't have anything specific in mind for anyone in particular (sound familiar—like the beginning of this book's story?). She quickly realized that you can indeed help people level up their speaking skills if they have these three things:

- An audience
- A location
- A date/time

when you can give a talk, speech, or remarks (of ANY length).

So find a time, place, and people to talk to. Define the genre. Imagine what question you can answer for them. Know your time limit. Imagine what the room will look like. And what your ask to them will be. What should they know, feel, or do? Then start building that speaking habit. Practice out loud, with your full voice and all your non-verbals and visuals. Record yourself and work through all the mess. Ask for help and then show up. Own that room and deliver the best you can in that moment. Then go ahead and do it again.

We know you can because speaking is not natural; no one was born speaking. We've all learned how to do it one gurgle, word, phrase, sentence, conversation, interview, group project presentation, board report, town hall, TED talk, graduation speech, conference keynote at a time. And you can, too.

When clients call in and say they don't have opportunities to speak in their career—they don't give regular presentations, they don't lead team meetings, they aren't asked to speak at conferences (yet)—we know that coaching them one-on-one will have limited success. After all, speaking, like any habitual practice, requires a regular time and place to build. You also need to have real audiences to speak to so you can wrestle with the social nature of speaking. And some of the most important feedback you can get comes after the delivery of your message.

So, if this is you, we recommend looking up your local Toastmasters chapter. Toastmasters has been around for nearly 100 years. As a non-profit organization, its network of clubs was created to help you gain the skills you need to become a confident speaker. Most importantly, if you look at it through the lens of the threshold concepts for speaking, Toastmasters gives you the time and place to practice in front of real people, truly embodying the practice and the mess of speaking. Their curriculum invites you to try out multiple genres of speaking, and they incorporate feedback into every meeting.

Ruth's father participated in Toastmasters before he went to law school, and it undoubtedly helped him get better so he was far more prepared when the day came for him to speak in his professional capacity. (In fact, the copper wine glass that they used to give out to those who completed the course for what was probably their celebratory "toast" sits in Ruth's office with "Bill Milligan, 1950, Toastmasters" engraved on it.)

## Scenario #2

You are a business or organization leader whose team needs to improve their presentation skills. Your team is VERY BUSY, with no time for formal training or coaching. Just getting stuff done is enough.

In a regular workplace scenario, your team meets weekly (or any other regularly occurring event), and you assign the speaking roles to your leaders. Instead, you could pass around the speaking roles to many more associates, giving them a chance to build a habit, practice embodying their ideas, have a real audience, understand the mess of organizing a message, and most importantly, getting real-time feedback.

Between 2015 and the present, nearly every quarter another organization entrusts us to help "broaden" the scope of who gets to speak at consequential meetings and conferences to (a) give more diverse ideas a platform, (b) give more diverse associates (meaning both diverse and at different levels/expertise areas) a chance to be seen and heard, and (c) give them real-time practice to improve their skills.

About 18 months ago, a Fortune 500 company came to us—their supply chain meetings were not going well, and people were neither getting the information that they needed, nor were they clear about the actions they needed to take as a result of the meetings. These meetings were a barrage of dense slides and data with no clear takeaways. The leaders were getting their information from their direct reports and then reporting out without having the context of the situation.

Originally, they asked us to fix their meetings, but that's not what we do. And we determined that the meetings were a symptom of a larger issue—they were missing a clear structure with which to communicate this particular information. Even more, they weren't trusting their younger associates to report out themselves. So we started at the top of supply chain management and took them through a communication masterclass that we built for them for this purpose.

Subsequently, each quarter, we have 10–12 of their associates go through our masterclass, working down through their various levels, ensuring that all of their supply chain, marketing, education, and even finance departments are able to present their own information in meetings clearly and concisely. They leave our class able to identify the highest value message, know how to keep the message tight, and they've simplified their slide content so people don't have to choose whether to read or listen. As a result, more people have a voice in their weekly meetings. They now focus on the headlines and the actionable items instead of spending time on unimportant details. We've essentially managed a culture change. And things are going much more smoothly as we train up more and more members of the team.

## Scenario #3

You are a high school or college instructor who wants to help your students prepare for the future. How do you find natural ways to tuck these into your curriculum without much effort? (Because we know you are already overwhelmed attempting to do everything.)

You define many different activities in your syllabus: papers, group projects, lab reports. You hold your students accountable for learning by assessments both small and large (quizzes, tests, exams). Take a step back from the entire year and ask how many times are students called on to speak their knowledge—both planned and/ or spontaneous. How many times can they support their peers in doing so? And how many times do you put students in the role of the "coach" where they are charged with being a feedback provider, not just a speaker to a specific task?

A few more specific ideas:

Turn a low-stakes quiz into a low-stakes video recording. Give them something to organize and say (not just write) within 90 seconds or less.

Create "short talk" events to replace a paper while classmates are also graded on their evaluation and feedback of the speaker.

Imagine students other than those in the student council making assembly announcements or (gasp) even graduation speeches.

Whether you are in the office or the classroom, take these three levels and see where you can adjust the opportunities for more speaking even slightly.

INDIVIDUAL:
Record on any number of devices or apps and listen back.

**GROUP:**

Assign a group presentation and require that all participants have equal time to speak. Do not let the shy associates or students hide behind the extroverted ones.

**PEER:**

Find chances for associates or students to present in small groups to their peers, with or without a leader or teacher listening in.

## Thresholds, in Summary

Since we named these threshold concepts for learning to speak, we start or end every coaching and training engagement explaining them. And through the course of our work with clients using this lens, we find three things:

- The threshold concepts continue to help us all see things in new ways, and we can start seeing them in practice everywhere. Meaning we can see them—and our clients see them—everywhere in the practice. This is why we find them so genuinely helpful.

- If a speaker continually struggles as a communicator, they are likely missing one of these concepts. As in, they aren't practicing the talk. Or their words are still on the page and not embodied. Or they haven't actually listened to themselves or asked for feedback.

- The concepts become influential over time. The practice toward being a great communicator will change. There is more tolerance when things get messy and uncomfortable, knowing it's a part of the process. Better questions are asked of meeting and event planners. Speaking to the listening, knowing how to gauge content against time and more become habitual and comfortable.

And again, we will never claim this is *natural*. All of what you learn when you encounter these thresholds will hopefully land you with some wonderfully confident habits toward the goal of being the best communicator and speaker you can be. We have seen the hard work pay off hundreds if not thousands of times. We wish you luck in your journey.

# Your Speaking Toolkit

The six threshold concepts you've come to understand are key to unlocking your communication potential. They fundamentally shape how you think about and approach speaking. This Speaker's Toolkit provides the practical skills, strategies, and technologies to help you along your journey. Whether you're working on core competencies or exploring the use of AI, these are the essential resources at your disposal for becoming a more effective communicator.

## Core Skills

### These are the practical skills required for any level of communicator

While we have offered you strategies to understand the threshold concepts for becoming a great speaker, it's time to dig into the actual skills required to be one. Core skills are behaviors that *can be learned.*

Some will require more practice than others; some will be more relevant depending on the genre, audience, and goals of the engagement. In this section, we address the ones most commonly accepted: vocal, verbal, non-verbal, and our fourth, emotional. Along the way we will give you a few exercises you can try to build each skill.

## Vocal

Vocal skills are about how words sound when they are delivered from your body, regardless of what words you are speaking. There are fields of study that dive deeply into the many components that make up the human voice. For simplicity, we break the vocal skill down into five main areas:

1. **Enunciation and Diction:** Pronouncing words clearly and distinctly. This means hitting your consonants, landing the ends of the words (hard d's, p's, k's, t's . . . ) and not slurring words together.

EXERCISE:

Pretend you have an apricot sitting in the middle of your tongue. Now try to talk around this invisible apricot without crushing it. You will sound pretty silly while you try it. If you still want to be understood, you have to really work to enunciate around that space. You might need to massage your jaw first to make room for that invisible apricot.

EXERCISE:

Chew your words. Really over-articulate—open your mouth, lift your cheeks, use your lips, feel ridiculous in it. Try recording this one to listen back. Chances are good that what feels like overdoing it to you will sound normal and clear to the people listening.

2. **Vocal Projection:** Speaking with the appropriate volume level so the audience at the back of the room can hear you (or in contrast, no one feels like you are yelling in the front of the room). Even if you are using a microphone, you want to use your full voice. Audio engineers will thank you for it.

EXERCISE:

As Patrick Swayze's Johnny says in *Dirty Dancing*, "No one puts Baby in a corner."[1] But sometimes we do. To help with your volume, stand in the corner of a large-ish room facing the corner. Start talking, and really listen to the volume of your voice as it hits the wall and bounces back to your ears. After you have a sense of what that sounds like, take one step back and keep talking. Try to keep the volume you hear the same. Every sentence or so, take another step back, maintaining the same volume level. Really tune into your ears—you'll get feedback from the room.

As you were stepping back, what did you do to keep it the same? If you can hear your voice hitting the walls and bouncing back to you, you will know you will be heard.

*If you are struggling with volume, especially if it is a new or recent problem, you may want to consider getting your hearing checked. The two can be linked.*

3. **Voice Modulation:** Variation in tone, pitch, speed, and volume to give interest to what you are saying. This is in contrast to monotonous speaking.

EXERCISE:

Speak the way you would read a bedtime story or fairy tale to a child. Really go for it—high energy, sing-songy. It may sound silly to you, but it may sound normal to listeners.

4. **Pausing:** Using strategic pauses for emphasis and clarity. In other words, can you tolerate a quiet moment for the audience to feel the weight of something important or just let them catch up with your rapid thoughts?

EXERCISE:

Read a paragraph from any book, ignoring the punctuation. Race through commas, dashes, semicolons, and periods. Maybe it doesn't feel that strange to you. Chances are good you'll start to slip back into reading to the punctuation. Then read it again, but this time, at every comma, take a brief pause, and at every period, take a full breath. Remember that to properly breathe before you speak, you need only inhale. If you exhale, you won't have any air to talk. Next, try to apply this to your speaking. Consider your punctuation, and take the time to breathe at the end of your spoken sentences.

5. **Controlling Breathing:** Positively underpinning every effective communicator's success is their ability to use breath to their advantage, not let lack of breath take control. This is particularly important for those who speak rapidly.

EXERCISE:

Lie on your back with your feet flat on the ground. Take 7–10 breaths and notice how your body expands and contracts. Then place your hands on your belly. Take 7–10 breaths as you focus on moving your hands. Notice how your stomach expands and your back pushes into the ground. These deep breaths are where we can take in the most air and are also calming. Then move your hands up to either side of your rib cage and take 7–10 breaths while allowing your ribs to fully expand with a thoracic breath. This is where our power comes from when we speak. Then take three breaths with your hands on your clavicle. Notice how little breath you can get here. This is where we breathe when we are panicked. Finally take 7–10 full breaths with no particular focus. Notice how much more you can get. You will need that breath to speak well.

EXERCISE:

Place the tip of your tongue on your gum (alveolar) ridge directly behind your front teeth and make a very light and sustained "s" sound. The "s" should be high in pitch, but you want to avoid sounding like air leaking out of a tire. If you put your hand in front of your mouth you will feel little to no air. Notice how your abdominal muscles gently and gradually contract in and up until you run out of air. Time yourself. At first you might only be able to maintain the "s" sound for 10–15 seconds. But if you practice this 1–3 times per day, you can increase your breath control by 2–5 seconds every week up to 40–50 seconds.

## Verbal

Verbal refers to the actual words you say, your content, regardless of how you say them. We set out not to repeat much of the good work that has been written on this subject, but instead, nod to those in the field who we believe have done it best. Before we share those authors and their expertise at the end of this section, we want to remind you that content takes on five main areas:

**Goal:** Defining a goal for your communication, or what you want the audience to do when they leave the room after your talk. Then aligning that goal with the perspective/ needs of the audience.

**Structure:** Organizing content logically and coherently so the audience can follow your ideas, data, and information.

**Storytelling:** Crafting and delivering compelling stories to engage the senses and ultimately lead your audience to emotion and feeling.

**Clarity of Language:** Using language that your audience will understand without including alienating jargon, and in ways that are concise and memorable.

**Visualization:** Creating vivid mental images for the audience to aid in telling your story. This may be through the spoken word or in accompanying slides/visuals.

Four books we love on the subject of organizing your own content:

*The Pyramid Principle*, by Barbara Minto. She is assuredly the dean of how to structure thinking to get to your highest value message. In short—how do you fit a lot of information into a concise communication? She answers this question most expertly.[2]

*The Story Factor* by Annette Simmons. There are MANY books on storytelling that we have read and like. But we really love Simmons' book as she walks through why, how, and where stories work with very practical applications.[3]

*TED Talks: The Official Guide to Public Speaking* by Chris Anderson. Truth be told, we like his short video that accompanied the solid but long book, if you just want the TL;DR. We were coaching TEDx talks for six years before he published his book so we had a pretty good idea how to help others in organizing their messages and stories like he suggests.[4] But the video "TED's secret to great public speaking" really can help bridge the gap of understanding: What sparks an audience to connect with your idea?[5]

*The Art of Public Speaking: 2023 Release, 13th Edition*, by Stephen Lucas, is one of the most popular textbooks used in college courses. While we know that a textbook can be cumbersome, Lucas's chapters on organizing messaging are succinct and helpful.[6]

## Non-Verbal

There are so many non-verbal qualities that impact how your message will be perceived. It can be overwhelming. Below you will find three main areas of non-verbals that we coach to every day. When you nail these, most other non-verbal qualities will follow. At the end we've included more books for your reference.

1. **Eye Contact:** In most cultures, we are taught from a young age to make eye contact when we speak to someone. Especially in Western cultures, this engenders trust and allows us to connect to our audience. In our new virtual and hybrid world, eye contact has a new set of rules. Connecting with the audience now may mean staring at a small camera at the top of your computer, or a camera at the back of a room that is recording you. When we're kids standing up to deliver our first speech in front of the class, our teachers often advise us to "scan the room." For some, this habit sticks. They make nothing more than fleeting eye contact, so no one in the audience really feels connected. We support the concept of steady gazes, not rapid eye scanning, for any presentation from a classroom to an arena.

EXERCISE:

To break the scanning habit, try making eye contact with one person at a time while sharing an entire point with them. Then switch to another person and share an entire point with them. As you truly engage with that person, everyone else in the room will feel that connection. For larger audiences, you can use the same technique but with zones rather than individuals: share one point with a small group on the right of the audience, then switch to the left, then to the back, and on and on.

2. **Body Language:** Using gestures and posture effectively. There is a technical term for how we use body language to communicate: *para-language*. Para-language helps convey meaning around the words you say. And we use it naturally and daily. We will refer to the book *Play the Part* for a deep dive in this specific skill set.[7] Our consistent default is "whatever gives you congruence in your message" is the body language to use. This also may mean cultivating a neutral stance.

POSTURE

A good neutral stance is built from the feet up:

Start with your feet directly under your hips—not too narrow to avoid tipping and lack of balance, and not too wide to prevent swaying and shifting your weight back and forth.

Have equal weight in each of your feet and send energy into the floor. Knees—keep them soft, unlocked. You don't want to cut off blood flow and pass out.

Keep shoulders rolled back, activating the space between your shoulder blades so your chest doesn't cave in.

You want your head resting gently atop your neck, avoiding a jutting chin. Imagine you have a string attached

to the crown of the head and it is reaching toward the
ceiling, expanding the space between each of your
vertebrae.

People have a habit of protecting the most vulnerable
parts of our bodies, our hearts and soft underbelly. But
you want to learn how to feel comfortable exposing
your most vulnerable parts: your stomach and heart.
Best practice is to have your hands gently hanging at
your sides or gently clasped at the belly button level
until you're ready to use them.

## GESTURE

Most speakers we work with will ask us: "What do I do
with my hands if they aren't in neutral?" The truth
is, most speakers don't need to focus too much on
this. When you're talking to a person one-on-one
you probably gesture without conscious thought.
Gestures come naturally to most people—as long as
they don't get caught up in the stress of the moment
and lock their arms to their side. If this is you, try
shaking your arms out; get nice and loose before
you speak.

If you want to be deliberate with your hands, here are
four tips:

1. Gestures that include an open palm will invite the
   audience in and help them to feel comfortable.

2. Gestures with palms downward indicate an
   emphatic point.

**3.** Pointing can be misconstrued in different cultures, so use it judiciously.

**4.** Gestures that are asymmetrical are less distracting and appear more natural than gestures that are the same on both sides.

**3. Movement:** You may have noticed that a good neutral stance doesn't involve pacing or moving very much. In fact, in the way we have described it to this point, there is stillness in a neutral stance, because we want you to focus on being grounded physically, and sending energy into the floor. You might think that pacing is a good way to expend nervous energy, but you're actually taxing your audience, asking them to spend energy tracking you instead of listening to your words.

That doesn't mean you can't move when you're delivering a talk or communication. If you're a natural mover, it's going to take you even more energy to stand still and your audience will notice how uncomfortable you are in stillness. If you need to move, consider these best practices:

**1.** Move only on a new thought or idea. When you start moving in the middle of an idea, it muddies the information.

**2.** Move with purpose. An important communication is held back by aimless movement, or moving for the sake of moving. Try this instead: Take a few steps. Plant your feet for a while. On a new idea and moving purposefully, take a few steps to a new space. Plant again.

This type of movement makes you more approachable, keeps you more grounded, and gives you better eye contact.

4. **Appearance:** How you look when you enter the room, even before you speak. Does your attire match the spirit and energy of your personality but not overshadow the dress code of the audience? Do your clothes fit—regardless of your size—and are they appropriate for the event genre and setting?

There are only three "rules" we recommend, no matter the genre:

1. Feel good in what you're wearing. If it makes you feel confident and doesn't restrict your movement, it's a good choice.

2. If you will be on-camera, avoid close patterns and small stripes that can move and distract on screen.

3. Wear shoes that are comfortable! And be sure they allow you to put weight through your whole foot.

Three books we love related to non-verbal communication:

*Play the Part* by Gina Barnett: As we mentioned before, this is a great book full of practical and sometimes silly exercises to try.[8]

*Executive Presence* by Sylvia Hewlett: Sylvia Hewlett was among the first to study what people meant when they said "Executive Presence." It's a great book that goes beyond speaking.[9]

*Presence* by Amy Cuddy: A pioneer of "power posing," Amy Cuddy turns her attention to how we can harness our own power and allow it to become visible.[10]

## Emotional Grounding

Emotions, as we've addressed, can hijack any communication. You can have the best voice, best message, and most well-poised posture and appearance and BOOM! Something can trigger you that brings you to your knees. Or, sometimes fear gets in your way from the very beginning, stunting your ability or even keeping you from speaking in the first place. There is no shortage of books on how to overcome your stage fright. From our perspective, the first step is to know your own stress response.

Stress responses come in four general "flavors." Each looks different when you speak. You have probably experienced each one of them at some point, but most people have one or two that are their go-to's when they are at work.

First, there's **fight**. You know this one. And while you can probably resist punching your co-workers, if you get caught in a fight response you might raise your voice or lean in and point. Or you might really dig your heels in and argue your point—so much so that afterward you wonder why you cared so much. These behaviors are the hallmarks of a fight response.

Then, **flight**. Flight responses don't usually result in running out of the room when things get tough in a presentation, although some people do try to get out of speaking any time they are asked. If you are in a flight response, you might rush through your words, cut content on the fly, or taper off at the end of your sentences. Sometimes you might even agree when you don't agree—anything to get it over with if you're in a flight response.

If you don't fight or flee, you might **freeze** under stress. This response is often accompanied by a lot of physiological clues: sweating, blotchiness, clammy hands, dry mouth. To be clear, any stress response can include these reactions, but "freezers" notice them. In fact, it might be all they can think about. Because the defining feature is that your brain seems to shut down or feel fuzzy—the only thoughts you might have are of how terribly you're doing. We've even seen speakers continue to talk while they are in a freeze response. But when you ask them what they said, they don't remember.

Lastly, the fourth stress response, **fawn**. Imagine a dog's behavior when it's done something bad. Her cute puppy eyes look up longingly, or he comes in close for a cuddle. For humans, fawning looks a lot like people-pleasing. It might sound like immediate agreement, or a sing-songy voice, or even excessive joking. And we don't mean jokes that are funny—think jokes where the teller is laughing first and loudest.

The first step of recovering from your stress response is recognizing that you are in one.

This can be tricky since sometimes fighting for your idea is the best strategy . . . if you have information that others are missing. Or cutting content might be a good idea . . . if your audience is way ahead of you.

But if you are not grounded when you make that choice, you just can't trust it.

There is a well-known quote that is often incorrectly credited to Viktor Frankl, and despite our best efforts, we cannot identify the original source. Despite this, we believe it is highly relevant for this learning:

> *"Between stimulus and response there is a space. And in that space lies our freedom and power to choose our responses."*

The best speakers know that when their stress response has been triggered, they must create space.

Most people have one or two ways they do this already—most of our clients do. But sometimes they just don't work. This is where we recommend practicing a 3-pronged approach to combating your stress response. We call them the 3 B's: body, breath, and brain.

**Body**  A quick way to get out of your stress response is to get back inside your body. While your brain might be freaking out, getting into your body can remind you that you're safe.

There are two good ways to do this. One is to take up space. Make sure you are sitting or standing tall with your feet firmly planted on the ground. This is particularly effective before you begin speaking.

The second way to get back inside your body is to focus on sensations. Try it now: wiggle your toes and really notice how it feels. Or put your hand on your desk and notice the temperature. Do you notice how your attention shifts? When your brain is overcome by a stress response, this can have a powerful effect.

There are a million ways you could get back in your body. We encourage you to find yours.


**Breath**   Breath is the foundation for everything we do. And yet when we are under stress, our breathing often becomes irregular and shallow.

When stress kicks in, simply stopping to take a breath is quick and works! You can increase its effectiveness by breathing deeply into your belly. Belly breathing has been shown to temporarily lower your blood pressure. It's that powerful.

You can also breathe in through your nose. This can really help slow you down, assuming you're not dealing with allergies.

When you have more time, like before you present, you can incorporate breathing exercises that take a bit more time. Box breathing is a great technique to try. Here's how it works: You breathe in for 4. Hold for 4. Breathe out for 4. And wait for 4. We use this exercise in many of our classes and it's amazing to feel how the energy of the entire room shifts after three short rounds of box breathing.

Again, there are many different techniques you could try using your breath. The important thing is to find what works for you.


**Brain**   Sometimes you need to talk back to your stress response to pull yourself out of it. Using the power of mantras or pep talks is a great use of our brain power.

A mantra could be comforting like, "You're okay."

Or maybe it's motivational: "You got this."

Or it could draw your attention outward, reminding you, "It's not about me."

Even "Just breathe" can be a mantra.

Over our time working with clients, we find that what works best is usually short, kind to yourself, and causes a physiological change. You just feel calmer when you think or say it. The phrases are also extremely personal—so you'll know it when you find it.

Now, these strategies are great for those in-the-moment experiences when you feel that stress coming on, but what about before you even get started? When you know you have a presentation coming up and the stress has set in well before you open your mouth? Anything you can do to ground yourself before you take the stage or the mic will benefit you.

You might pump yourself up with a great playlist, or have a dance party of one to get your body moving and the blood flowing.

You could tap into the power of positive self-talk. Before she took the floor for her final routine of the day at the 2024 Olympics, gymnast Suni Lee was captured on camera talking to herself. She was preparing her mind by telling herself, "Okay . . . you got this . . . last one . . . this is for me . . . last one ever . . . come on . . . without a doubt . . . "[11] What words would build your confidence?

Any of the breathing techniques above are also easily incorporated before you speak. Box breathing is our personal favorite—it's a great one to really slow yourself down.

Perhaps you are someone who meditates. If you're not, it's a great way to get your brain and breath working for you instead of against you.

And we have a favorite body tip for you that is truly effective (and has some science to back it up). If you are a Ted Lasso fan, you might remember how Rebecca coached Nate and Keeley when they asked her what she did to feel really confident. She threw her hands up high and wide, opened her stance, opened her face up, stuck her tongue out, and did a lion's breath.

Essentially, she was power posing, an idea Amy Cuddy shared in her 2012 TED talk. She found that taking a big stance, like that of Wonder Woman (feet wide, hands on your hips in fists) or Superman (feet wide, one hand on your hip, the other pointed to the sky), or any wide and big stance (think WWE wrestlers) will affect your hormone levels. Her research showed that when you do this pose for two minutes, your cortisol (stress hormone) drops and your testosterone (courage hormone) increases.[12]

Can't find a quiet place to power pose for two minutes? Sit upright in your chair with your feet firmly planted on the floor, pushing into them. Put your hands on the arms of your chair, elbows up and wide.

You may feel silly doing it, but at the very least you will feel the tingle in your limbs as the blood gets moving. And anything you can do to prepare your body and brain for a stressful experience is worthwhile.

## Advanced Skills

Once you have mastered the core skills, these advanced skills can be achieved for more sophisticated engagements and proficiency. In this section, we will address self-awareness, humor, facilitation, and inclusiveness.

### Self-awareness

This may seem obvious. But trust us, it isn't. Knowing one's strengths and weaknesses as a speaker comes only with all of the threshold concepts in play: building habits, embodying your talks, knowing the mess, understanding different genres, deeply appreciating the social/audience component, and really, above all, always seeking feedback.

Often, you also carry history and memory from your last engagement(s), which can be helpful or distracting. Some speakers struggle to overcome a terrible failure, which prevents them from any improvement. Relying on your strengths but knowing you always have something to improve is a healthy place to start. Other speakers never celebrate their successes, however incremental, so they don't realize that they are improving.

*TIP: Always be a learner to continually increase your self-awareness.*

### Humor

Humor is hard—really hard. It's not something that's easily taught and comes with a lot of advanced skill and practice.

But when used properly, humor can be a highly effective shortcut to getting an audience's attention and engagement.

A client we worked with, let's call him Jack, is a supremely nice man. He's also a CEO who still wants to be "one of the boys" in his male-dominated company and industry. He tries to do this by making jokes. The problem is, he's a nervous speaker. His anxiety leaks through, and the jokes just don't land. The audience senses his discomfort, and becomes a little uncomfortable. Any giggles are unsure, and poor Jack breaks out in a sweat like a comedian having a rough night. So, until he can really ground himself for those jokes, we encourage him to focus on his audience and connect with them, rather than trying to make them laugh.

*TIP: Be sure you are a master of emotional grounding before you add humor.*

### Interactivity

When we imagine a person who incorporates a lot of interactivity when they speak, we think of a facilitator. This may be a podcast host, TV interviewer, or training facilitator.

While facilitation is a specific genre of speaking, it requires knowing how to engage your audience through questions or activities.

Additionally, a good facilitator needs to modulate their energy to bring their audience along. Do you level up your energy to try to lift a sullen, skeptical audience? Or do you meet them where they are? Knowing how to "index" your passion and enthusiasm is central to being received effectively.

*TIP: You need masterful listening to truly excel here.*

## Inclusiveness

At one of Ruth's keynotes, she asked if anyone "didn't know what pie was," being overly cautious about her examples. Someone indeed raised their hand and said, "We don't eat pie in our culture." But indeed, they had pie charts. Inclusiveness is being aware of and adapting to cultural or social sensitivities.

Acacia once facilitated a workshop where seven different native languages were represented. While everyone spoke English, she needed to adjust or explain idioms. Another speaker we worked with needed help understanding that his point of view as a privileged white man did not welcome the diverse experiences and perspectives of his team.

*TIP: Work on building your empathy for this advanced skill.*

# Technology and Speaking

It's hard to be a professional anything these days without the use of technology. In this final chapter, we will review our best practices for developing and speaking with slide visuals and live demos.

We will also address the growing number of AI tools promising to help you be a better speaker. Spoiler: they can't, without understanding the threshold concepts and your dedication to practice.

## On Using Slides

We're talking about PowerPoint, Keynote, Quarto, Google Slides, Canva, and any new apps we don't know the name of yet . . . in other words, any visual presentation.

Let's set this up: You have been invited to present and asked to bring slides because . . . everyone else speaking has slides.

Does that mean you *need* slides? (Not necessarily.)

Does that mean you open up a slide deck to start your presentation? (No, no, *please* don't ever do this.)

Does that mean you know how to design them so they don't look like the intersection of clip art meets a wall of 10-point font paragraphs? (Most likely not.)

Does that mean the culture at your organization expects the PowerPoint to be a read-ahead, leave-behind, or serve as a memo or email? (Absolutely.)

Does that mean you know *how to decide what earns the right to make a slide?* (The million-dollar question!)

If you are reading this book, you assuredly desire to improve your communications. But in your 10, 20, or more years learning or working, it's probably accurate to say you haven't had any formal training in PowerPoint. Very few people have.

And while we don't expect everyone to be a graphic designer, the following are the guidelines we share with all our clients. They are best practices that can help you understand the true purpose (or the *why*) behind using visuals, the best design rules, and some usage tips. We refer you to a few other worthy references for a more in-depth review of actual slide design in the "For More Study" section.

These "how" instructions are written for easy consumption and adoption.

Our bottom line to slide development and design:

*Remember that your audience cannot read and listen to you at the same time.*

Brevity of words, avoiding large blocks of copy and overstuffed slides, will help your audience better engage with your content and message.

**The Purpose of Presentation Slides**   Presentation slides are an essential tool for delivering information and engaging an audience. They serve several key purposes:

- **Engage audiences:** Visuals, when used effectively, can capture the audience's attention and help them connect with the narrative being presented.

- **Evoke emotion:** Visuals can elicit emotional responses, making the presentation more memorable and impactful.

- **Clarify complexity:** Complex ideas or data can be simplified through visual representations, making them easier to understand.

- **Keep/regain audience attention:** Visual elements help maintain focus and prevent the audience from becoming disengaged.

- **Share pathway/agenda:** Visual agendas provide a clear roadmap for the presentation, helping both the speaker and the audience stay on track.

- **Distill key points:** Slides should highlight the most important takeaways, reinforcing the core message of the presentation.

**Slide Design Guidelines**   To create effective slides, it's important to follow some key design guidelines:

- **One concluding thought per slide:** Each slide should have a clear and concise takeaway message.

- **One dominant image:** Use a single, high-quality image to reinforce the main point of the slide. Avoid using multiple images or clip art, as this can clutter the slide and distract the audience.

- **28-point font minimum/limited text:** Ensure that the font size is at least 28 points for easy readability. Keep the text concise and to the point, using only essential keywords and phrases.

- **Avoid bullet points:** Bullet points encourage reading and can be visually unappealing and overwhelming. Instead, use visuals or concise sentences to convey information.

- **Limit animation:** Use builds or clicks sparingly to focus the audience's attention on specific elements of the slide. Excessive animations can be distracting and detract from the message. Avoid using flying or swirling animations, as they can appear unprofessional and outdated.

- **Whitespace:** Utilize negative space effectively to help the audience focus on the key elements of the slide. Cluttered slides can be confusing and overwhelming.

- **Simple graphs:** Keep graphs clean and easy to understand. Choose one type of data visualization to avoid confusion.

- **Appropriate video usage:** Ensure that any videos used add value to the presentation and are well-rehearsed. Involve the on-site AV team early on to avoid technical difficulties.

- **Consistency is key:** Maintain consistency in design elements such as font, font size, backgrounds, headlines, and colors throughout the presentation. This creates a professional and cohesive look.

- **Know your projector dimensions and test for contrast:** Ask about the projector dimensions beforehand and format slides accordingly. Test the slides on the projector to ensure that images are displayed with the correct color and contrast.

**Speaking with Slides**  Delivering a presentation effectively involves more than just having well-designed slides. Here are some key tips for speaking with slides:

- **Clear and Preview:** Before clicking to the next slide, ensure you've covered/cleared all the content on the current slide, then give the audience a verbal preview of where you're heading next. This helps maintain a smooth flow and prevents the audience from feeling lost.

- **Look at your audience, not your slides:** Avoid looking at the screen behind you. Instead, use a confidence monitor or find a way to maintain eye contact with the audience.

- **Don't speak over any audio or video:** If your slide contains audio or video elements, pause and let them play without speaking over them. This allows the audience to fully absorb the information being presented.

- **Only use builds, no pointer:** Use builds to reveal information gradually, and avoid using a laser pointer, as it can be distracting.

- **Explain graph components:** If you include data slides, take the time to explain each component of the graph clearly. This helps the audience understand the data and its significance.

**Technology Reminders**   Many slide decks are viewed on TINY screens—since people are often attending virtual meetings on their phones. Make sure to imagine what your design would look like at 20% of what you see on your desktop.

Expect something may go wrong with the projector, your computer, the electricity, or your mouse/clicker. Prepare a backup plan with a thumb-drive or file saved in the cloud. Have your notes separate from the PowerPoint so you can still deliver your talk without slides if all technology falls down.

## On Live Demonstrations (Portals, Coding)

Hadley Wickham, one of the world's most notable authors and programmers for R (the programming language for data and analytics), engages us for the annual conference of his company, Posit. We coach their many presenters (think nearly a hundred) every year to help the conference become one of the most accessible and engaging events on the data/analytics industry circuit. Hadley and Ruth jointly give the orientation and their first requirement is: you gotta have a really good reason, *like really really good*, to do a live demo.

When your presentation includes a "live demo" like coding, a website, or portal tour, we have one very complete thought: *don't*. At least don't do it live. Let us count the reasons why and offer a few ways to achieve the same goal as a live demo.

Why to avoid it:

The risk is high that something will go wrong. The internet drops. A 404 error. Live code doesn't perform properly. A client asks you to click on a button you weren't planning to show. You waste the audience's time and attention trying to recover in any of those scenarios.

How to avoid it:

Aim for the "look live" option of a pre-recorded tour or code demo. Plenty of options exist for this solution from screen shots threaded together to apps that will capture your navigation in a re-watchable video.

## On Using AI Feedback Applications

The whole AI craze is getting pretty real, isn't it? And we're just as curious as the next person about how best to use AI to make our lives better, easier, and improve what we do. There are a plenitude of apps showing up purporting to help you with your speech clarity and promising to make you a better speaker. Some of them might be really good and might work well based on what you're looking for.

Initially, we were going to rank them, but it's pretty subjective, and we're not TechCrunch or The Verge. You might be looking for an app that is going to focus specifically on your filler words, varying your intonation, or even how to time content when presenting with slides. As a result, we don't want to tell you which ones you should use (assuredly dating ourselves and this book given the lifecycle of new apps), but we do want to offer you some guidance on *when and how* you might best use them.

Keep in mind that when you get third-party feedback, regardless of whether it comes from a tool or a human, it is most useful when:

1. It's aligned with your goals as a speaker.

2. It's aligned with the perspective of your audience.

3. It comes at the right time in the process and in the right format.

These recommendations come from first-hand reviews by a focus group we assembled of university communication students, their professor, and some clients on apps currently available at the time of publishing.

**What Do They Do Well?** They allow you to practice. Sometimes all you need is time and space to get in reps. Most of these apps give you exercises that you can use to practice in a no-stakes environment. And that can make a difference! Especially if you're not getting opportunities for that at work or in other areas of your life.

The exercises range from massaging your jaw, to articulating specific words to improve clarity, to creating an impromptu speech based around an image the app provides. There are videos of professionals leading exercises, and others are written descriptions of exercises, so the amount of input you receive to do the exercise well varies.

**They are a good source of feedback.** Some of them can tell you how many times you say "um." Some of them can measure pitch and volume. Some of them can measure speed of speech and clarity. Some of them can tell you if you sound "masculine" or "feminine." (We aren't exactly sure what that means or how that's measured, but it's a measure.)

**What Don't They Do Well?** They can be a bad source of feedback. We hate to break it to you, but AI isn't really thinking about high-level feedback yet. Overall, these apps don't allow for input into the *type* of communication you're making or what might be necessary for that genre, setting, or goal. As a result, you'll get feedback from these apps, but you will have to filter it to know what is useful for you based on what you're trying to accomplish.

In our minds, the danger is that you receive feedback and it doesn't tell you what to do about it. Or you don't know how to interpret it. Either one is going to leave you feeling stuck. Like, *I know I have this bad habit, but what do I do now?* In this case, we encourage you to ask a human. Get a second opinion. Get confirmation that they are hearing the same thing the app is identifying. Ideally, that human is part of your intended audience and has the specificity of giving you feedback from that perspective.

**Nuance.** What we truly notice about these apps is that they don't understand or read nuance very well. For instance, if a communication moment, like a meaningful story or a call to action, requires you to change your pace or your volume, these tools will likely flag the change as a negative. We've run into this ourselves in the Microsoft Teams speaker coach—it's always telling us to slow down right as we are getting excited about something in a call.

**Arbitrary Scoring.** Some of these apps assign scores to your ability without giving specific reasoning behind the scores. Arbitrary scoring and unclear criteria don't really help you learn. Often the onus is on the user to interpret the data you're receiving. But if you're seeking information, instruction, and guidance on how to improve, these tools may leave you wanting more.

**Timing Matters.** *When* you use the tools matters. We are not talking about what time of day (although one app does ask you what time of day you prefer to practice). Think about using an app when you don't have something important coming up, when you're curious or you're working on development. If you lean on them in the stressful time before you deliver a communication, they could potentially add to your stress or derail your preparation. Consider your motivation to use these tools. Are you motivated to try it when you don't have an important communication on the horizon?

**The Bottom Line**  Proceed with optimistic caution. They may help you practice, but they won't solve anything for you. If you do use the tools, and discover a bunch of disfluencies or challenges that you don't know how to address, reach out to a human. AI tools are a great way to start, but call in the professionals when something important is on the line.

# Speaking Personas

Do you see yourself? Do you have any habits that need addressing?

Here you will find the fairly comprehensive, entirely unscientific, assembly of "personas that speakers might embody." Admittedly, we have a lot of fun with these, and really, you should too. We love to name them as it brings clarity to the *why* someone behaves in a certain way when speaking and helps them to normalize that (a) they aren't alone and (b) it's likely something they need to address. We might also call this list the "habits you need to unlearn" before you can expect to dominate any stage. Or, not so elegantly, the list that makes someone call us for help.

Truth be told, we all might find ourselves slipping into these personas under different circumstances. Each is totally human. And sometimes these behaviors become habitual. So much so that we might not even recognize them in ourselves. As we have spent years getting to know (and love) the people behind each of these archetypes, we have come to deeply appreciate the work that needs to be done to overcome them. And even though skills and tips and tricks might help, ultimately, only by wrestling with one or all of the threshold concepts can a speaker avoid these pitfalls.

Under each persona, we've listed the specific threshold concepts they are distinctly not understanding.

## The Externally Focused Speakers

**The Hustler** You know this person; usually they are in sales. They are always selling *something*. Often over-selling too. Selling has a special place and it's rarely from the stage. But if there is an ask, make it at the end and make it quick.

*Social, Genre, Feedback*

**The Beauty Queen** assuredly is confident but has a challenge when with a live audience. They are often trained to smile and look between audience members, not at them. In the practice of "speaking to the listening" this poses a fundamental problem. We don't see it often, but are able to help when we do.

*Habit, Embodied, Feedback*

**The Preacher** As it sounds, someone who wants to tell you what to do. In our years of coaching TEDx talks, there was always one word that was the "preacher tell" and that was "should": "You should do this, you should do that." We gently suggest replacing that word with "invite." We invite you . . . not to use the word "should."

*Social, Genre, Feedback*

## The Deep Thinkers

**The Magpie** You know that cute long-tailed crow that likes to collect things? So does this speaker. They are insatiably curious and continually gather more content or feedback beyond the real need. This presents a challenge when they are told they have double the content for the amount of time they have, and they have a harder job of editing to the expectation. We often say, "Remember the difference between what *you* may need and what the *talk or speech* may need."

*Habit, Social, Genre, Feedback*

**The Recycler** The speaker that comes with an old deck assuming it will work for a new audience. We give this person a very simple suggestion at the start of an engagement: "How about you put that deck aside for a minute and tell us a little about your new audience, goal, and question you are answering. It's likely we'll go back to the slides in a bit." And we rarely do.

*Habit, Social, Genre, Feedback*

**The Reader** "Please, please read us all the dense text from your slides," said no audience ever. This person reads a script, or worse yet, the full paragraphs that made it onto slides. Our plea to this person is: do not read your text unless you are a professional writer and you are reading an excerpt from your novel on a book tour.

*ALL: Habits, Messy, Social, Genre, Embodied, Feedback*

**The Writer** Okay, this may be someone who ends up reading, too. But a writer is someone who wants to spell out every word they expect to say. They struggle to make the leap into embodiment. This often doesn't end very well since, as we've explained, we don't write like we speak. When a writer tries to stand up and speak without their script, they find themselves tripping over their words as they try to find the "perfect" ones they wrote.

*Messy, Genre, Social, Embodied*

**The Perfectionist** We can identify one of these a few ways. One sees the audience as a threat and has a stress response even when prepared. The lack of control they have over the outcome causes blotchy necks, dry mouths, and sweaty hands. The other perfectionist is the person who insists on practicing, revising, practicing, revising for even the smallest of talks. The last one got a 4.0 from second grade through college. They aren't used to making mistakes. This is a good reminder that great is the enemy of good. Especially for the audience that isn't fully listening. They just want to know your clear, concise message and that they can trust you.

*Habit, Messy, Embodied, Feedback*

## The Subject Matter Experts

**The Professor** Academics' superpower and also their kryptonite: they have a *lot* of information to share. A question we pose mostly in this category is: How much information does your audience need to believe something is true? We love their knowledge, just not 100 pounds of it in a 10-pound bag.

*Habit, Social, Genre, Feedback*

**The Policy Wonk** uses a plethora of strategy words and acronyms to explain the programmatic directive of the long-term plan aiming to impact the sustainable development of, well, of course, policy. The LTPISDP, duh! (representing ALL acronyms we are supposed to know but don't—like this one which is entirely made up). While all of those are important, we usually aim to bring a human element to the policy. We can imagine what Susan looks like in her healthy life with her complex Medicaid benefits, but the continuum-of-care-management-program-ten-point-plan that cares for her is not very memorable.

*Habit, Messy, Social, Genre, Feedback*

**The Clinical Scientist** doesn't realize they aren't in their lab anymore talking to peers. When that scientist is invited to present their ideas to a lay audience, the rules of preparation and delivery change. The list is long but always starts with "What question does the audience have?" and "How can I answer it without losing them in my charts, graphs, and scientific jargon?" For the record, we never ask anyone to dumb down their science, but instead, make it *accessible*.

*Habit, Messy, Social, Genre, Feedback*

**The Data Scientist** has an abundance of *logos* (not the graphic kind, either) but needs to dig for the *pathos*. In other words, plenty of facts but not enough emotion and story. We coach more data scientists than any other professional category, so we have a special place in our hearts for them. But we still work hard to remind them that live demos are never a good idea, either. Go for the "look live" and you won't get the 404 error message or spinning wheel of death, ever.

*Habit, Messy, Social, Genre, Feedback*

## The Speakers Who Just Can't Stop

**The Filibusterer** Admittedly, we think of this word in legislative settings, but similar behavior also shows up in boardrooms and executive leadership meetings. The presentation might start with someone who is knowledgeable, but at some point, their own fears and insecurities take over. They over-communicate simple ideas, giving too much data or repeating points. Their "pauses" for questions are never long enough for anyone to speak. The result is an audience that feels beholden to listen and fear some pushback if they try to give constructive feedback—before or after the presentation. Like in a filibuster, there is little listening to the audience, only speaking at them.

*ALL: Habits, Messy, Social, Genre, Embodied, Feedback*

**The Windbag** A speaker who has won over the audience but keeps on going long past their audience's need or attention span. And repeats the ending many times! Again, someone who likes to hear themself talk. One cure is to learn to use a clock and honor the contract with the audience to not go over time. Another might be to plan your final sentences and practice them diligently.

*ALL: Habits, Messy, Social, Genre, Embodied, Feedback*

**The Monologuer** They might as well be in a room all alone. This person speaks without acknowledging the audience, or inviting them to participate or react. Their nonverbals are restrained and rarely do they look up from their notes. We have yet to meet an audience who would want to hear this person speak.

*ALL: Habits, Messy, Social, Genre, Embodied, Feedback*

**The Firehose** If there is one image we want people to imagine when they are speaking, it is not a firehose. The image we prefer is an oscillating sprinkler, the kind that gently cascades you with elegant streams of water, then gives you a break to enjoy the mist and not be waterboarded. A firehose is someone who shoots a high volume of forceful water at you with no pausing or chance to process what has been said. For the record, we don't mind people speaking quickly at us because really, who wants to listen to a Kin-der-gar-ten-tea-cher-paced-de-li-very? What we mind, what everyone minds, is when speakers don't take pauses to break up sections of messages or stories, or to let people connect for a minute with something they may already know. Firehoses leave floods of information with no audience considerations.

We have three main strategies for these people and they are breathing, breathing, and breathing.

*ALL: Habits, Messy, Social, Genre, Embodied, Feedback*

## The Unicorns

**The Riffer** Someone who likes to share ideas, but has little license to do so. This may be someone with a lot of opinions who just loves an audience. Chances are good you haven't been asked to do your stand-up set. Often, you don't get invited back if you are a riffer, so there's not much opportunity to try again. Just show up with good data and story whenever possible and you won't fall into this trap.

*ALL: Habits, Messy, Social, Genre, Embodied, Feedback*

**The Adrenalizer** Remember the classmate who would cram for exams the night before? The adult version of them is not much different. This person habitually procrastinates or avoids preparing and therefore relies on adrenaline to carry them through. This leads to a lot of hits and misses in speaking. And the misses will be obvious to an audience because there are fumbles (especially in the beginning and end) and they often go way too long since there's been no rehearsal or feedback.

*Habit, Feedback*

**The Avoider** The person who tries to get out of any speaking engagement and never builds habits or skills. We don't have many suggestions for this persona. As we referenced earlier, the first thing you have to do to learn to catch a football is want to catch that football.

*Habit (gotta start somewhere!)*

**The Spy** This is our shorthand for the person who doesn't want to be vulnerable or share who they truly are. What gives them license to influence us? Ruth remembers a speaker who gave a remarkable talk on a highly complex topic but didn't explain at all who he was. She said in a kind way, "That was a great talk, but . . . who are you?" and he replied offensively, "Don't you know?" Enough said.

*Embodied, Feedback*

If you recognize yourself in any of these personas and are eager for change, you are ready to pursue this persona:

## The Motivated Speaker

The is the person who understands the necessity of building a speaking habit of practice, embraces the mess of building a message that resonates, who interrogates event genres, pursues full embodiment in their delivery, and is willing to ask for and receive feedback. This speaker is limitless.

# Conclusion: On Practicing

Former First Lady Michelle Obama shared a simple mantra she would tell her daughters during an interview: "You have to start practicing who you want to be."[1]

Throughout this whole book, we have shared the underpinnings to being a great speaker and communicator. But we know at the end of the day it isn't what we write, think, or say; it is what you do.

And as we tell all of our speakers, you must close out every talk, presentation, or speech with a call to action. What do you want your audience to do, feel, or believe? And invite them to do just that.

So here is ours, to no one's surprise: practice.

Here are a few hints that can help make your practice salient and productive:

1. You will make the most improvement or change *when you are ready to change*. If you are distracted, reluctant, and tired, that isn't a good time to try.

2. The best time to try to improve *is when you have an event on your calendar*—meaning a time, place, purpose, and audience that is expecting to hear from you. Positively nothing is more motivating than the adrenaline you feel leading up to a live moment. With real people staring back at you. With a time limit. With a promise to your audience that they will leave with more knowledge or feeling about a topic than before they heard from you.

3. Understand that *training* and *practice* are different. If you are trying to train a part of your voice to do something different, that is like learning a new serve in tennis. A coach is likely standing next to you making real-time corrections on your toss, body position, and follow-through stroke. You may have a before-and-after video that solidifies the visual of what you were doing wrong and then proves you *can* make the correction. Listening to yourself and making a correction, also recorded, is the gold standard of training. You then take that new skill and put it into practice with repetitions before it is the regular way you do it.

4. Don't miss out on the small moments (like a one-to-two minute report at a staff meeting)—use that as a chance to practice—like a quiz in a class, without a lot of consequence but the chance to try. As we know, it's the habits that build over time that allow for better long-term performance. No athlete or actor expects to show up to game day or opening night ready to go without a lot of small, incremental tries beforehand.

5. Always ask for feedback *before you speak*. Take a quick look back on our advice on asking for the right feedback from a prepared person. Never ask anyone how you did only after you speak. We assure you, most people don't want to hurt your feelings and will simply say, "You did great."

# You're a Motivated Speaker . . . Now What?

Whether you are a novice or seasoned speaker, the threshold concepts in this book will unlock possibilities and deepen your impact as a communicator. We believe you can improve your ability when you pair your understanding of principles with consistent behaviors. While this book contains many practical strategies, we've assembled many more to help you on your journey as a motivated speaker.

You can access these resources at

TheMotivatedSpeaker.com/book

# Our (Speaking) Origin Stories

When our speakers are trying to come up with a poignant, concise story to demonstrate the license they have to influence an audience, we ask this simple question:

*"What was the time and place you knew this would be your life's work?"*

So we turned that question on ourselves to share with you, our readers, about what brought us to this book.

## Ruth

There were 8 people on stage at a theater inside The Ohio State University and 300 people in the audience on a Tuesday in October 2009 for the first-ever TEDxColumbus and only the 35th such TEDx event across the globe. After working tirelessly for six months on the event, I had a reflection I could not shake.

Why did most of the speakers do well on the stage, but some others, not so much?

I had done my best work at trying to support each of them leading up to the event, but only having been a speech writer, I was a little short on tricks at being a speech coach. I will never forget one speaker showing up to rehearsal the day before with a slide deck that was a merger of two entire talks she had given before, and when she delivered them, the talk was a good 12 minutes over the time limit. *Gulp*.

I went looking for someone to help me with the next year's speakers. TEDx as a movement was still in its infancy and hadn't built out speaker coaching resources yet. I knew I didn't want a speechwriter for the speakers, as I wanted each of the speakers to own their own content, story, and delivery. I also didn't want a media trainer only telling them how to repeat three key messages over and over.

So I spent the next year figuring it out. I reference a story in the book of when Amy Barnes, a professor from OSU, and I documented the process so that future students could amply coach tenured professors. With that in hand, I ended up being one of the longest continuous TEDx organizers until, like a lot of things, COVID brought us to a close. It is still one of the most treasured experiences of my career, creating more meaningful experiences and friendships than any job could offer.

I looked back on my entire career and realized this thing with TEDx wasn't that surprising. My father used to take me to endless Rotary club meetings and other speeches he wanted me to hear—including many of his own. As a litigator and legislator, his command of language had a profound impact on me.

The first A I *ever* got was in Public Speaking at Miami University. I then decided to major in speech communication in large part due to a wonderful professor, Paul Mongeau, who saw me for who I was—a curious, non-grade-motivated student. (I found him at Arizona State University these 34 years later, gleefully on a sabbatical when we asked him to give feedback on this manuscript, which he did—adding immense value.) After Miami, I became a speechwriter in politics, and then pursued a variety of communications jobs until I narrowed my PR practice to only do public speaking coaching and training. This has brought me, and my team who have traveled this incredible journey with me, to this place today—where you are reading this book.

## Acacia

I often say that, before I joined Articulation in 2016, I led a double life. I spent my days as a facilitator and coach, helping others to learn, grow, and achieve great things. By night, I was acting and directing professionally. (Truth be told, I've always had this tendency toward the "double," studying theatre performance and economics in college.)

I loved both of my "lives"—onstage and at work. And in January 2016, I took a leap. I left my corporate role and struck out for . . . I didn't exactly know. The only thing I knew was that I wanted to bring my two worlds together. I wanted to be whole.

I found my spark in a piece of text that I first encountered my senior year in college. It was another time when I was wondering what I was going to do with my life. Fretting and wondering how I would make a difference in the world. That's when I saw a movie, *Waking Life* by Richard Linklater. It would change my life.

There's this moment when one character says to another:

*"When I say 'love,' the sound comes out of my mouth and it hits the other person's ear, travels through this Byzantine conduit in their brain, through their memories of love or lack of love, and they register what I'm saying and they say yes, they understand.*

*But how do I know they understand? Because words are inert. They're just symbols. They're dead, you know? And so much of our experience is intangible. So much of what we perceive cannot be expressed. It's unspeakable."*

I felt this in the core of my being—this longing to be understood. Maybe you do, too. And the distance between our experience and what we can express can feel untenable. To put yourself out there and try to connect with another person is vulnerable and full of risk.

So why open your mouth at all? The scene in *Waking Life* goes on to say:

*"And yet, when we communicate with one another, and we feel that we've connected, and we think that we're understood, I think we have a feeling of almost spiritual communion. And that feeling might be transient, but I think it's what we live for."*[1]

In 2003, as I was leaving college, these words (which I eventually got to say on stage) gave me courage to pursue a life in the arts. I spent years on stage learning how to bridge that gap of understanding, and ultimately, help audiences to connect with another person's words and experiences. It's an extraordinary feeling to say something and feel that you have deeply connected to another person whom you have never even met. I feel lucky to do that with my art.

And in 2016, as I embarked on a new path (that led me to Articulation), I realized that I could help other people have this same experience. As an executive communication coach, I get to help speakers share what they believe, what they know, and what they care about, and then to savor the thrill and deep satisfaction when someone else truly understands them. Even if it's only for a moment.

I believe that human connection is a powerful force. It is what provides meaning to our lives and, at our core, what we all yearn for. So, even though it's transient, even though it can be difficult, and filled with risk, I encourage every person I work with, and you, dear reader, to know that what you say matters. And, with effort and practice, you can truly feel understood. And it's so worth it.

## Blythe

*"When a man's verses cannot be understood . . . it strikes a man more dead than a great reckoning in a little room."*

—As You Like It, *Act 3, Scene 3*

I was in my second year of a 3-year MFA in Acting program before I really understood Shakespeare. That wasn't for lack of trying. At that point, I already had a BA and an MA in English Literature. I should have loved and appreciated Shakespeare. Instead, I hated it. Mostly because I didn't get it.

Then John Basil, my classical acting professor, walked into my life.

He was warm, soft spoken, with sparkling eyes and a boyish sense of play. And he made Shakespeare make sense. He was the first person who ever told me that Shakespeare was never intended to be read. While there were printed versions of his plays, Shakespeare was writing his plays for a largely illiterate society, so he intended them to be seen and heard in the middle of the day in a rowdy setting like The Globe. Which explains so much about how he wrote them!

John shared with my class that everything we need to know is there in the text—all of the emotion, all of the stage directions, all of the things that Shakespeare intended us to convey—Shakespeare included it all in there. But it was our job as performers of Shakespeare to make the words make sense. Which meant that even to learn it and understand it ourselves, we really needed to be saying the words out loud and hearing what they sounded like. And beyond that, it was up to the audience to make sense of what we did with those words. I made it my mission that other students of Shakespeare didn't feel like I had—to make sure they understood the power of the *spoken* word of Shakespeare.

Now, after working with these threshold concepts for speaking, I find myself feeling the same way I did about teaching Shakespeare. His texts are a perfect example of the difference between words written on a page and those spoken into the world, and how we make meaning so differently from them. I love that my work once again is about turning people from haters into believers, or at the very least helping people to feel more comfortable speaking their speech[es]. I love guiding clients through choosing their spoken words carefully, helping them wring the most meaning they can from the words they share with an audience. I want each of my clients to know the value of their story, of the words they choose to put into the world, and just how powerful those words can be.

# For More Study

$B$ooks from our shelf we think should be on your shelf:

*Freeing the Natural Voice* by Kristin Linklater. This is perhaps the most widely used text on the voice in actor training. Its focus is on reconnecting speakers with their natural voice by releasing physical and psychological tension.[1]

*Permission to Speak* by Samara Bay. Samara is a voice coach to movie stars and political luminaries. Her approach to the voice is both practical and inspiring. She invites the reader to reconsider what "power" sounds like.[2] We read it together as a team and enjoyed her unique lens and storytelling.

*The Use and Training of the Human Voice: A Bio-Dynamic Approach to Vocal Life* by Arthur Lessac. If you can't tell by the title, this is a more academic book. But our coaches go back to it time and time again to build up a speaker's ability to use their voice, particularly to understand how to take full advantage of the music of language.[3]

*Speak without Fear* by Ivy Naistadt is the standout title for us on overcoming fear. There are so many titles in this space (around speaking fear) but Ivy's perspective and writing are most accessible with practical tips we have used and know work.[4]

*Play the Part: Master Body Signals to Connect and Communicate for Business Success* by Gina Barnett. Gina's work with TED speakers and this book are the gold standard for understanding how your body, non-verbals, and paralanguage get used and trained for great speaking delivery.[5] It is one of our most dog-eared books on the shelf.

*Resonate*[6] and *slide:ology*[7] by Nancy Duarte (and her subsequent titles) and *Everyday Business Storytelling*[8] by Janine Kurnoff and Lee Lazarus are three books that can bring curiosity to the visual process of storytelling through slides.

*TED's Guide to Public Speaking*[9] by Chris Anderson has a special place on our shelf thanks to all of our TEDx and TED-like training, but we also find his short video on what makes a TED talk a TED talk the essence of the book and through his own spoken live narrative. We have shown it dozens, if not hundreds, of times to clients.

*Think Faster, Talk Smarter* by Matt Abrahams, and his podcast *Think Fast, Talk Smart* are a terrific resource for navigating spontaneous genres of public speaking. Abrahams outlines six steps to becoming better at speaking off the cuff, which help speakers build good habits even for unprepared moments.[10]

# TED Talks

Anderson, Chris. "TED's Secret to Great Public Speaking." TED Studio, Mar. 2016, https://www.ted.com/talks/chris_anderson_ted_s_secret_to_great_public_speaking

Edmondson, Amy. "How to Turn a Group of Strangers into a Team." TED, Nov. 2017, www.ted.com/talks/amyedmondsonhowtoturna groupofstrangersintoateam

Headlee, Celeste. "10 Ways to Have a Better Conversation." TED, Mar. 2015, www.ted.com/talks/celesteheadlee10waystohavea betterconversation

Joseph, Dr. Ivan. "The Skill of Self Confidence." YouTube, uploaded by TEDx Talks, 16 Jan. 2013, www.youtube.com/watch?v=w-HYZv6HzAs.

McWhorter, John. "Txtng Is Killing Language. JK!!!" TED, Feb. 2013, www.ted.com/talks/johnmcwhortertxtngiskillinglanguagejk

Treasure, Julian. "How to Speak So That People Want to Listen." TED, June 2014, https://www.ted.com/talks/julian_treasure_how_to_speak_so_that_people_want_to_listen

# Notes

## Introduction

1. Meyer, J.H.F., and Land, R. 2003. "Threshold Concepts and Troublesome Knowledge: Linkages to Ways of Thinking and Practicing with the Disciplines." *Improving Student Learning Theory and Practice — 10 Years On* (ISL10): 412–42. Oxford Brookes University.
2. Ibid.

## Chapter 1

1. Etymonline.com. 2024. "Confidence (n.)." Updated October 13, 2021. https://www.etymonline.com/word/confidence.
2. Telecaster, source unknown.
3. Gawande, Atul. 2009. *The Checklist Manifesto: How to Get Things Right*. Metropolitan Books.
4. Clear, James. 2018. *Atomic Habits: An Easy & Proven Way to Build Good Habits & Break Bad Ones*. Avery.
5. Covey, Steven R. 1989. *The 7 Habits of Highly Effective People*. Free Press.

# Chapter 2

1. Frost, Robert. "A Servant to Servants." North of Boston. David Nutt. 1914.
2. Holiday, Ryan. 2014. *The Obstacle is the Way: The Timeless Art of Turning Trials into Triumph*. Portfolio.
3. Minto, Barbara. 2010. *The Pyramid Principle: Logic in Writing and Thinking*. Pearson Education.
4. Wilson, Margaret. 2002. "Six Views of Embodied Cognition." *Psychonomic Bulletin & Review* (9): 625–636.
5. McWhorter, John. "Txtng Is Killing Language. JK!!!" TED. February 2013. Video, 13:34. https://www.ted.com/talks/john_mcwhorter_txtng_is_killing_language_jk.
6. Echelman, Janet. "Taking Imagination Seriously." TED. March 2011. Video, 9:09. https://www.ted.com/talks/janet_echelman_taking_imagination_seriously.
7. Barkley, Russell A. 2012. *Executive Functions: What They Are, How They Work, and Why They Evolved*. The Guilford Press.
8. Petz, Jon. 2024. Phone call with Ruth Milligan. September 10, 2024.
9. Simmons, Annette. 2000. *The Story Factor: Inspiration, Influence, and Persuasion through the Arts of Storytelling*. Basic Books.
10. Smith, Paul. 2012. *Lead with a Story: A Guide to Crafting Business Narrative That Captivate, Convince, and Inspire*. AMACOM.

# Chapter 3

1. Luntz, Frank. 2007. *Words That Work: It's Not What You Say, It's What People Hear*. Hachette Books.
2. Adler-Kassner, Linda and Elizabeth Wardle. 2015. *Naming What We Know: Threshold Concepts of Writing Studies*. Utah State University Press.
3. Musk, Elon. 2018. "Tesla (TSLA) Q1 2018 Results — Earnings Call Transcript." May 3. https://seekingalpha.com/article/4169027-tesla-tsla-q1-2018-results-earnings-call-transcript.
4. ESPN.com. 2020. "Reds Suspend Thom Brennaman for Using Anti-Gay Slur on Air." August 19, 2020. https://www.espn.com/mlb/story/_/id/29699199/reds-broadcaster-thom-brennaman-uses-anti-gay-slur-air.

5. Goodman, Paul. 1971. *Speaking and Language: Defence of Poetry*. Random House.
6. Treasure, Julian. 2011. Live workshop attended by Ruth Milligan.

# Chapter 4

1. Biden, Joseph. 2024. "Biden Addresses Debate Performance at Campaign Rally." Speech presented in Raleigh, NC, June 28, 2024. YouTube. Last modified June 28, 2024. https://www.youtube.com/watch?v=IEYONiZWjJc.
2. Parker, Priya. 2018. *The Art of Gathering: How We Meet and Why It Matters*. Riverhead Books.

# Chapter 5

1. McCroskey, James C. 2017. *An Introduction to Rhetorical Communication: A Western Rhetorical Perspective*. Taylor & Francis.
2. Hopkins, Brian. 2019. "Performance (linguistics)." *Lancaster Glossary of Child Development*. Effective May 22, 2019. https://www.lancaster.ac.uk/fas/psych/glossary/performance_-linguistics/.

# Chapter 6

1. Smith, Larry. August 2024. Email to Ruth Milligan.
2. Hattie, John and Helen Timperley. 2007. "The Power of Feedback." *Review of Educational Research* 77 (1). 81-112. https://www.columbia.edu/~mvp19/ETF/Feedback.pdf.
3. Hart-Davidson, Bill. 2023. "Have We Ever Done A Good Job Teaching Writing?" Medium.com, September 6. https://billhd.medium.com/have-we-ever-done-a-good-job-teaching-writing-1d4e87e138b5.
4. Edmonson, Amy C. 2018. *The Fearless Organization: Creating Psychological Safety in the Workplace for Learning, Innovation, and Growth*. Wiley.
5. Ibid.

# Chapter 7

1. Wardle, Elizabeth. 2019. "What Critics of Student Writing Get Wrong." The Chronicle of Higher Education, August 30. https://www.chronicle.com/article/what-critics-of-student-writing-get-wrong/.

# Chapter 8

1. Ardolino, Emile, dir. 1987. *Dirty Dancing*. Great American Films Limited Partnership & Vestron Pictures.
2. Minto, Barbara. 2010. *The Pyramid Principle: Logic in Writing and Thinking*. Pearson Education.
3. Simmons, Annette. 2000. *The Story Factor: Inspiration, Influence, and Persuasion through the Arts of Storytelling*. Basic Books.
4. Anderson, Chris. 2016. *TED Talks: The Official TED Guide to Public Speaking*. Houghton Mifflin Harcourt.
5. Anderson, Chris. "TED's Secret to Great Public Speaking." TED. March 2016. Video, 7:46. https://www.ted.com/talks/chris_anderson_ted_s_secret_to_great_public_speaking?subtitle=en.
6. Lucas, Stephen and Paul Stob. 2023. *The Art of Public Speaking: 2023 Release*. McGraw Hill.
7. Barnett, Gina. 2015. *Play the Part: Master Body Signals to Connect and Communicate for Business Success*. McGraw Hill.
8. Ibid.
9. Hewlett, Sylvia Ann. 2014. *Executive Presence: The Missing Link between Merit and Success*. Harper Business.
10. Cuddy, Amy. 2015. *Presence: Bringing Your Boldest Self to Your Biggest Challenges*. Back Bay Books.
11. NBC Olympics & Paralympics (@nbcolympics). 2024. "Suni Lee recited affirmations to herself before crushing her floor routine. #ParisOlympics #TeamUSA." TikTok, August 1, 2024. https://www.tiktok.com/@nbcolympics/video/7398359651504393518.
12. Cuddy, Amy. "Your Body Language May Shape Who You Are." TED. June 2012. Video, 20:45. https://www.ted.com/talks/amy_cuddy_your_body_language_may_shape_who_you_are?subtitle=en.

# Conclusion

1. Obama, Michelle. 2018. "Michelle Obama & Tracee Ellis Ross in Conversation at the 2018 United State of Women Summit." YouTube. May 5, 2018. Video, 41:30. https://www.youtube.com/watch?v=boB9modnMYQ.

# Our (Speaking) Origin Stories

1. Linklater, Richard, dir. 2001. *Waking Life*. Fox Searchlight Pictures.

# For More Study

1. Linklater, Kristen. 2006. *Freeing the Natural Voice: Imagery and Art in the Practice of Voice and Language* (Revised & Expanded). Drama Publishers.
2. Bay, Samara. 2023. *Permission to Speak: How to Change What Power Sounds Like, Starting with You.* Crown.
3. Lessac, Arthur. 1994. *The Use and Training of the Human Voice: A Bio-Dynamic Approach to Vocal Life.* McGraw Hill.
4. Naistadt, Ivy. 2004. *Speak without Fear: A Total System for Becoming a Natural, Confident Speaker.* Harper.
5. Barnett, Gina. 2015. *Play the Part: Master Body Signals to Connect and Communicate for Business Success.* McGraw Hill.
6. Duarte, Nancy. 2010. *Resonate: Present Visual Stories that Transform Audiences.* John Wiley & Sons.
7. Duarte, Nancy. 2007. *Slide:ology: The Art and Science of Creating Great Presentations.* O'Reilly Media.
8. Kurnoff, Janine and Lee Lazarus. 2021. *Everyday Business Story-telling: Create, Simplify, and Adapt a Visual Narrative for Any Audience.* Wiley.
9. Anderson, Chris. 2016. *TED Talks: The Official TED Guide to Public Speaking.* Houghton Mifflin Harcourt.
10. Abrahams, Matt. 2023. *Think Faster, Talk Smarter: How to Speak Successfully When You're Put on the Spot.* Simon Element/Simon Acumen.

# Acknowledgments

This book is the direct result of the generosity and genius of Elizabeth Wardle. It simply would not have happened without her.

Jointly, we are indebted to Kim Goldsmith, Helmut Berthold, and Michelle Bretscher, who supported us in every step from a random spark of curiosity to a published book. They are the backbone of our daily work.

Thanks to Phillip Marino, Purvi Patel, Zach Schisgal, and Debbie Williams from the Wiley team, who brought so many pieces together to make this book a reality. Thank you for taking a chance on us. Likewise special thanks to Jim Minatel, Larry Smith, and Betsy Allen, who all provided invaluable counsel early in the process. And lastly to Ruth's first speech professor, who stoked her passion at Miami, Paul Mongeau, who, 35 years later, provided us incredible feedback on the manuscript. What a full-circle gift.

The work of Articulation would also not be possible without our key business partners in Susan Rector, Linda Cosgray, Cary Hanosek, Kristin O'Keefe, Eden Sulzer, and Alan Jazak.

While we dedicated the book to all the speakers with whom we've had the honor of working, we give special thanks to our clients who hire us consistently. There aren't enough pages to list you here.

**From Ruth:**

From the origin of TEDxColumbus, which was the moment I knew I wanted to do this "speaker" work, I'm grateful to Nancy Kramer, Lara Stein and the team at TED, our TEDx collaborators, and so many brilliant speakers.

To all of my Miami University colleagues and friends, who were central in creating connections that led to our curiosity, study, and writing that resulted in this book.

To every single professional champion who has hired me, been our partner, or just given the right piece of advice at the right time, thank you. This book is an artifact of those decades of support and advocacy.

To my sisters Edie and Martha who tolerated me as the little one; to Mom for her love of the perfect Scrabble word; and to my beloved dad, Bill Milligan, who really was my original spark with his deep love of ideas, a hearty dinner conversation, and especially the oratorical process. Dad, your 1950 Toastmaster's flute will sit next to a copy of this book.

Most importantly, I am blessed to have my husband Dave and children Maggie and Joseph walk with me each step in this life; I love you more than you can imagine.

**From Acacia:**

To my artistic home, Available Light Theatre, where I get to "live the life of the imagination." You teach me that when you lead with joy and care, you can make a difference.

I've been blessed by people who saw my potential. To Julia Guichard for revealing the power of my voice. Rebecca Roberts, Dawn Schenck, Holly Piddock, and Stephanie Anderson, thank you for elevating me as a leader and trainer. Artie Issac, thank you for your invaluable mentorship, guidance, and friendship.

Thank you to Michael, my big brother; to my dad, who brought out my exuberance and humor; and my mom, a trailblazing woman in leadership—all those late-night chats taught me the value of my words.

Finally, to my husband, coach, and biggest supporter, Matt Slaybaugh, thank you for showing me that love is an action. Every day, I face the world with confidence, knowing you have my back. You are my everything.

**From Blythe:**

Many thanks to Artie Isaac and Matt Slaybaugh, for helping me identify my strengths and find my way to what feels like the perfect job.

Much love to my parents, who always sent me to the dictionary during dinner conversations and told me that as long as I could communicate clearly, I could do whatever I wanted; and love and thanks to my husband Jim, who encourages and helps me to continue honing my skills every day.

# About the Authors

## Ruth Milligan

Ruth Milligan helps people find their voice, tell their story, and have their message be heard. For more than three decades, she has served as a communication strategist, coach, and trainer. Founder and curator of one of the longest-running TEDx programs, TEDxColumbus, her career has included roles of speechwriter, national press secretary, and embedded consultant to billion-dollar contract pitches for Fortune 10 companies.

Ruth received her BA in Speech Communication from Miami University. Prior to founding Articulation in 2010, which focuses exclusively on executive communication coaching and training, she ran a PR and marketing firm and worked in political and non-profit communications.

She has a deep connection and commitment to her forever home, Columbus, Ohio, where she has served on a variety of non-profit boards, and helped to launch the nation's third women-founded bank in town, Fortuna. She keeps active ties to Miami, having just finished a term on the university's foundation board.

In her spare time, Ruth plays a healthy amount of pickleball, and enjoys working out, biking, and hiking with her husband, Dave. They have two college-aged children and a dog, Bean.

## Acacia Duncan

Acacia Duncan trains speakers to captivate their audiences with purpose, precision, and passion. She helps leaders, CEOs, and experts to transform complex ideas into communications that shift perspectives and inspire action.

In one-on-one coaching, small-group settings, and workshops for 400+ people, Acacia equips professionals with tools for communicating confidently and persuasively. She also elevates company cultures by creating innovative training programs for businesses.

In addition to being the Director of Coaching and Training at Articulation, Acacia is a founding Company Member of Available Light Theatre. She is a professional director and actor who has performed in more than 60 plays and 3 feature films. Her decades of experience—on stage and off—have taught her how to bring out the creativity in every collaborator.

Before joining Articulation in 2016, Acacia spent 14 years as a corporate coach and trainer in the retail sector. She graduated from Miami University with degrees in Theatre Performance and Economics, studied at the London Academy of Music and Dramatic Arts, and received her coaching certification from Erickson Coaching International.

Acacia lives in Columbus, Ohio, with her husband, Matt Slaybaugh. She is a hiker, a baker, a dog-lover, and a life-long Trekkie.

## Blythe Coons

Blythe Coons is a communications coach who loves helping clients uncover their powerful stories. She coaches cohorts of influential conference speakers, leads masterclasses to unlock clear, concise communication, and elevates individual clients to bring their best selves to important keynotes and presentations. At Articulation, she is dedicated to helping others amplify their voices, connect authentically, and deliver messages that inspire action.

Across professional roles, Blythe has always been focused on clarifying complex messages. Armed with a BA from Haverford College and an MA from Middlebury College, she taught high-school students English literature before completing an MFA in Acting. For a decade, Blythe connected with audiences from the stage in professional theaters throughout the US, including the American Shakespeare Center.

Since returning to Columbus, Ohio, Blythe has served in leadership roles across steel fabrication, hospitality, and legal and financial services. She also devotes time to non-profit organizations that use storytelling to convey their mission.

Blythe enjoys baking the perfect treat for friends and family, running every morning, and hiking beautiful trails with her husband and two teenage step-children.

# Index